SOUTHERN INDIA

SOUTHERN
INDIA

WITH 50 COLOURED ILLUSTRATIONS

PAINTED BY LADY LAWLEY
DESCRIBED BY F. E. PENNY

GYAN

Published by

GYAN

Gyan Publishing House
5, Ansari Road
Daryaganj, New Delhi-110002
Phone: 011-47034999, 9811692060
E-mail: books@gyanbooks.com

Distribution Network
gyanbooks.com
India, USA, Canada, UK, Australia, France

ISBN : 978-81-212-4055-0 (PB)
First Published, London, 1914

2nd Impression 2020

Printed at: Gyan Press, Delhi.

Southern India
Author: F. E. Penny

THE MUHARRAM, A MUHAMMADAN RELIGIOUS FESTIVAL

The procession of the tabuts or taziahs through Triplicane, the Muhammadan quarter of Madras. The people beat their breasts and mourn aloud in commemoration of the deaths of Ali and of Hussain and Hasan, the prophet's son-in-law and grandsons.

SOUTHERN INDIA

PAINTED BY LADY LAWLEY · DESCRIBED BY F. E. PENNY · PUBLISHED BY A. & C. BLACK · LONDON

Published October 1914

CONTENTS

CHAPTER I

PAGE

Government House and the Mount Road, Madras . 1

CHAPTER II

Triplicane High Road and Some Ascetics . . . 13

CHAPTER III

The Muhammadans of Triplicane 27

CHAPTER IV

Muhammadan Marriage 39

CHAPTER V

The Faith of Islam 51

CHAPTER VI

Muhammadan Festivals and Superstitions . . . 69

CHAPTER VII

PAGE

Disease, Devils, and Devil-Doctors 81

CHAPTER VIII

Muhammadan Belief in Heaven and Hell 93

CHAPTER IX

Hinduism and Caste 105

CHAPTER X

The Hindu Village School and Temple 119

CHAPTER XI

Devil-Dancing 135

CHAPTER XII

The Hindu Homestead 151

CHAPTER XIII

Village Amusements 171

CHAPTER XIV

The Nilgiri Hills 189

CHAPTER XV

PAGE
The Gum Tree and the Forest 209

CHAPTER XVI

Mysore and Seringapatam 223

CHAPTER XVII

Canarese and Gipsies 241

INDEX 253

LIST OF ILLUSTRATIONS

1. The Muharram, a Muhammadan Religious Festival . . . . *Frontispiece*

FACING PAGE

2. A Jemadar of the 20th Deccan Horse 1
3. Adam, the Head Coachman at Government House, Madras 4
4. The Cook at Government House, Madras 8
5. A Trooper of the Governor's Bodyguard 11
6. Muniswami, the Government House Head Butler . 14
7. A Saddhu 19
8. A Learned Ascetic 22
9. A Muhammadan Child of Noble Birth 35
10. A Dhurzi or Tailor: a Muhammadan 38
11. A Khazi (Qazi), Muhammadan Magistrate . . . 43
12. A Muhammadan Girl 46
13. The Daughter of a Rich Muhammadan Merchant . 49
14. Syed Shah Fakhrud-deen Suf, a Muhammadan Munshi 56
15. A Muhammadan Officer 65
16. A Muhammadan Lady 72
17. A Muhammadan Boy 97

FACING PAGE

18. A Slave Girl in a Rich Muhammadan Family . . 104
19. A Hindu Pariah Beggar 115
20. Old Pariah Woman begging 118
21. The Car Festival at the Hindu Temple of Myliapore. 131
22. A Hindu Dasi or Nautch Girl 134
23. A Devil-Dancer of South India 147
24. Thomas, Lady Lawley's Personal Péon or Attendant 150
25. A Village Scene in Kalbundipore, Mysore . . 153
26. A Tamil Girl dressed for a Visit 155
27. A Pariah Woman 158
28. A Hindu Woman 160
29. A Corn Merchant 163
30. A Betel-Leaf and Areca-Nut Seller 166
31. A Barber 169
32. A Hindu Musician playing on a Tambour . . . 176
33. A Hindu Musician 179
34. The Vegetable Market at Ootacamund . . . 182
35. A Hindu Musician with a Cymbal 185
36. A Man belonging to one of the Forest Tribes of the Western Ghats 192
37. A Hindu, probably of the Bird-Trapper Tribe . . 201
38. A Man belonging to the Toda Tribe. 203
39. A Man of the Budaga Caste 206
40. A Canarese Water Woman 208
41. A Canarese Woman 211
42. A Tamil Pariah Woman 214
43. Early Morning on the Lake, Ootacamund . . 217

FACING PAGE

44. A Tank in Mysore with Canarese Women drawing Water 224
45. A Primitive Water-Cart of Mysore 227
46. A Mahratta Brahman Girl 230
47. A Tank in Mysore with the Maharajah's Palace in the distance 241
48. A Canarese Woman grinding Millet 243
49. A Woman of the Tribe of Indian Gipsies known as Lumbadi 246
50. A Canarese Woman drawing Water 248

Sketch Map at End of Volume.

A JEMADAR OF THE 20TH DECCAN HORSE

A troop of native cavalry is quartered in Madras for extra escort duty when the Governor is in residence at Government House.

GOVERNMENT HOUSE AND THE MOUNT ROAD, MADRAS

The yoke is where the gods place it.

Hindu Proverb.

CHAPTER I

GOVERNMENT HOUSE AND THE MOUNT ROAD, MADRAS

INDIA is a land of contrasts. They are not far to seek. They stand out with startling vividness side by side in the streets of every large town. Poverty and wealth, squalor and splendour, the twice-born Brahman and the despised outcaste move together in the broad highway, never touching each other as they pass, nor mingling their lives. Poverty devoid of pride humbly steps aside, holding out the suppliant hand as splendour, mounted on an elephant or Arab horse, rides by. The outcaste Punchama, considered too degraded to tie the shoe-string of the caste man, shrinks under the shadow of the wall as the Brahman strolls on his way in the middle of the street. However thronged the road may be with traffic, the Brahman has no fear that he will be run over or jostled; for it is well known that the unfortunate person who causes the death of a Brahman must expiate his sin by myriads of re-births on this earth, wherein he will find little joy and much sorrow.

Yet the Brahman does not have it all his own way. The street may be used by the Muhammadan, who regards every man not of his own faith as an infidel and therefore contemptible; or by the European, who brings a good-natured indifference to the East which the oriental has never understood.

There is no greater contrast than that which is experienced on leaving the gates of Government House in Madras. The change is felt in the scene and moral atmosphere. The park in which the house stands—with its deer, its flowers and shrubs, its peaceful retirement—is exchanged at the very gateway itself for a wide dusty street full of life and noise.

The street is bordered by portia trees that bear a pale yellow tulip-shaped blossom. They grow readily and love the sea air; and their bright green foliage is pleasant to look upon; otherwise the portia is not altogether a desirable avenue tree. The banyan and tamarind are more graceful and give a deeper shade.

Under the trees not twenty yards from the

ADAM, THE HEAD COACHMAN AT GOVERNMENT HOUSE, MADRAS

He is a Tamil Hindu. He is wearing the red and gold livery of the Governor's service.

gates may be seen the hawkers of rice-cakes, bananas, oranges, betel-leaf and areca-nut. Ten yards farther on squats a Valluvan, the astrologer and humble doctor-magician of one of the many hamlets of which Madras is composed. A bullock-cart with tired cattle halts under the very wall of the park. The bulls eat their provender of rice-straw, and the driver buys himself a rice-cake and a banana of the vendors near him.

Along the road pass bullock-carts, horses and carriages, motors and bicycles, ponies and jutkas—the two-wheeled conveyance of the country—and a constant stream of pedestrians. No one hurries in the East: yet for all that the drivers shout and gesticulate as they flog and goad their poor harried beasts, as if everything depended on the saving of time.

The soft red dust from the laterite road rises like powdered ochre and turns golden in the afternoon sun. The sea-breeze comes in from the Indian Ocean bringing with it the soft undertone of the falling surf; it brushes up the rustling fronds of the palms with a promise of refreshing coolness. The Cooum River that bounds on one side the Government House grounds, is spread in sheets of silver over its muddy bed. In the brackish water grows a weed that sets free the noxious phosphates of the mud. The air is polluted with a smell which even the double jasmine and Persian roses in the gardens cannot dominate.

The Governor's carriage passes out with its servants in scarlet liveries, its prancing horses and its dignified coachman, whose likeness Lady Lawley has caught in her sketch. The equipage is accompanied by an escort of the bodyguard—selected native troopers in red uniforms with glittering steel accoutrements and pennoned lances. The cavalcade clatters by; the red dust dances madly in the sun, and every eye is turned to follow the gorgeous sight until it is swallowed up in the golden haze of the Mount road.

Muniswami, the butler, is left standing on the top of the steps of Government House. In his way and among his people he is an important person. He is the head of the domestic establishment, which he rules over with the strong hand of a despot. He has seen a long succession of notable Governors and notable guests at the Governor's table. He understands the importance of his position, and maintains the dignity of it with acknowledged gravity. Butlers in private families pay him the highest compliment by imitating his manner and his tone.

One and all from the highest to the lowest are full of a curious wonder as they gaze after His Excellency; but this attitude does not spring from any feeling of envy. Among all classes there is covetousness of wealth and a desire to possess it; and this is shown in the usual ways of robbery and over-reaching; but the envy of social position is unknown in a country that is fast bound in the inexorable fetters of the caste system.

No one, from the Brahman passing along the road at his ease to the pariah widow selling betel-leaf and areca-nut under the portia trees, envies the Governor his high position; no one grudges him his brilliant escort of Lancers, his horses and carriages, his palace with its pillared verandahs and spacious rooms nor his numerous servants. But all alike, from the Brahman downwards, would have no objection to dip a hand into the Treasury chest, that the Governor helps to control.

Caste and the doctrine of fatalism in India combine to keep the units of humanity in their places, and to promote a contentment and resignation at which the European never ceases to marvel. Advocates of progress gird against the paralysing influence of caste. Were caste broken down to-morrow there would still be fatalism to deal with. "What is written on a man's forehead cannot be rubbed off," say Hindu and Muhammadan alike. The Governor's fate has to be fulfilled to the letter. Rich as he seems to be and surrounded by magnificence, he cannot escape the fate "that is written on his forehead" and relegate his duties to any other person. He is as much bound to his position by birth and circumstances as the widowed betel-vendor is compelled by birth and circumstances to sell her wares just outside Government House gates.

The Governor has gone; the extra cloud of dust raised by the tramp of the escort's horses settles down to its normal condition of haze; the attention of the staring open-mouthed people returns to the business of the day: they pass on; and we are left to watch the ways of the East on the high road.

One of the peculiarities of an Indian city, whether in the north or south, is the mixture of races that is to be seen at all times of the day. Possibly there is the same admixture in London, Paris, or Vienna, but it is not so marked, so obvious. It would be extremely difficult in Piccadilly to distinguish the different nationalities.

THE COOK AT GOVERNMENT HOUSE, MADRAS

He carries a brass tray of flowers, his offering at the shrine of his Hindu deity. He is a Tamil of South India.

Unless the ear caught the sound of the tongue, the eye could not decide with any certainty whether this man was a German and that a Frenchman. On the contrary, a Spaniard might be mistaken for an Italian, and a Greek for a Jew.

In an Indian city the identity of each nationality is plainly written on face and figure. The most casual observer can distinguish between a Muhammadan and a Hindu, an Afghan and a Singhalese, a Mahratta and an Armenian, an Arab and a Burmese; yet they are all of an oriental complexion and Asiatic type.

Among the Hindus themselves a distinction is visible. The Brahman and the Muckwa fisherman, the chetty and the syce, the coolie labourer and the clerk serving in a shop or office, the purohit or temple attendant and the domestic servant, are each to be recognised at a glance. Trade and caste have their marks and signs by which their followers may be known; and it may be said with certainty:

"There goes an Afghan; he has come from the far north with horses; he has sold them for money, which he will lay out on some product of the south that finds a ready sale up north—sandalwood oil, pearls, or perhaps a consignment of more bulky goods that will be sent by rail."

"Here comes a road coolie, a Wodiga by caste. He wears an unbleached loin-cloth bound tightly round his sinewy body, and an apology for a turban on his shaven head. Following at his heels are his wife and two daughters. They wear silver and brass ornaments set with shells instead of gems. They have been carrying baskets of laterite on their heads all day for road-mending; for that is their trade."

"There stands a Muhammadan. He has been sitting at the tailor's board in one of the little shops behind the English Club. All kinds of needlework are undertaken in that tiny den, from a ball-dress for an English lady to a chintz betel-bag for the horse-keeper's wife."

They all tell their tale of country, occupation, and, in most cases, of their faith as well. The Afghan trader and tailor are followers of the Prophet. The Hindu merchant, by the marks on his forehead, is a worshipper of Vishnu. The fisherman is a Christian belonging to the church founded in India by Xavier. The coolie and Wodiga are animists, and propitiate devils with blood sacrifices. The Singhalese is a Buddhist.

A TROOPER OF THE GOVERNOR'S BODY-GUARD

A fine corps of picked men drafted from other regiments of native cavalry.

From the lines drawn horizontally on his forehead the Hindu clerk proclaims himself a follower of the god Siva.

The oriental has no false shame about the profession of his religion. He exercises it without restraint, and respects the practice of it in others, whether they are of his own creed or of any other faith. This trait was exemplified at the visit of the King-Emperor, George V., to India. He openly observed Sunday as became a Christian; and attended the church service regularly. The action was regarded by the natives with approval; and His Majesty was honoured for his fidelity to his God. So impressed was a Sikh chief that he sent a gift to the church which the King attended in recognition of his sovereign's profession of faith.

TRIPLICANE HIGH ROAD AND SOME ASCETICS

Cakes are baked in a buttered dish, but rice is beaten in a pounder. Each must submit to his fate since it is apportioned by the gods.

Hindu Proverb.

MUNISWAMI, THE GOVERNMENT HOUSE HEAD BUTLER

A well-known character, who has served many Governors, and waited on Lord Roberts, Lord Dufferin, and many other celebrated English guests at Government House. He wears the old-fashioned Mahratta petticoat dress, which has been retained at the Madras Club as well as at Government House.

CHAPTER II

TRIPLICANE HIGH ROAD AND SOME ASCETICS

THE history of the present Government House in Madras has been written. When the East India Company first settled at Madras, the merchants in the service of the Company occupied a small fort, the original Fort St. George, on the sea-shore near the mouth of the Cooum River. They felt the heat of the shadeless coast and suffered in consequence, as the old burial registers testify.

The only form of punkah known was the large fan swung by a servant. The houses inside the Fort walls were constructed with more thought of defence than of obtaining fresh air. The stagnation and warmth of the atmosphere must have been terrible. No wonder that thirty-five years later we find them begging for permission to build "two or three chambers for the sick in the physick garden." The two or three chambers gradually developed into what was called the Company's

Garden House. It stood on a raised spot west of the Fort, and became in course of time the country house of the Governor.

The French were responsible for the change of site. They levelled the old Garden House to the ground during their occupation of Fort St. George, 1746–49. Historically it was a loss. The original building had seen a long succession of Governors. It was associated with Yale and Pitt, and is mentioned in the letters of the latter. Pitt was interested in the garden itself, and made experiments with vegetable seeds sent out from England.

When Madras was restored to the English in 1749, it was thought advisable by the authorities not to rebuild the house on the old site. It was too close to the native town, and there was no longer any necessity to be so near the Fort walls. The Governor in Council decided to buy the residence of a Portuguese merchant which was in the market. The house stood on the banks of the river south of the Fort, and about a mile from it; and it formed the nucleus of the present handsome building.

The first few years of its new ownership saw troublous times. The mansion fell into the hands of the French under Lally in 1758; it was much damaged, but not completely destroyed as was the old Garden House. In 1759 the siege of Madras was raised and the house recovered; but there was no money available for its repair. What money there was had to be spent for other purposes. It was made habitable and that was all.

It was not till the beginning of the nineteenth century that the Governor's residence began to assume its present proportions. The Banqueting Hall was built and additions were made to the house. In 1860 a third story was added and the park considerably enlarged by enclosing a part of the garden that had belonged to the Nawab of the Carnatic.

When the property was first acquired the Triplicane high road extended from the bridge over the river near the house to St. Thome in a direct line. It ran through the park, and its track may be distinguished by the avenue of old trees still standing. The road was diverted into what is now known as the Mount road.

Along that ancient way went the stream of humanity, passing from north to south, or south to north. The Afghan, whose destination was the pearl fishery of Tuticorin, stopped to rest in Triplicane, and obeyed the call to prayer from the mosque. The Hindu merchant with his bales of cotton goods did pujah at the temple in Myliapur close to Triplicane, and passed up the road on his way to the big towns of the north. Under the shade of the old trees, where the deer now feed, sat the orange and banana sellers, the vendors of betel-leaf and areca-nut. Weary travellers rested on their journey, and shifted their loads on to the raised stones set up for the purpose by former philanthropists.

The high road ends abruptly against the wall of the park, where the Wallajah road cuts it at right angles, and conducts the traveller into the Mount road. This spot has been the haunt of generations of wandering ascetics, who are venerated by the people and regarded with superstitious awe. Long before the advent of the English they sat at the cross road ready to be consulted and willing to receive alms. In receiving alms an ascetic, who has performed vows and acquired merit, confers a favour. With the gift the donor passes on his sins, and the Sadhu takes upon himself the consequences of the evil-doing of the giver. He is the scapegoat; but his stock of merit is so great that he escapes punishment and goes scathless.

If there is no necessity for a scapegoat, the

A SADDHU

One who has lived under vows, performed ascetic ceremonies, and become a sanyasi. He has thus acquired sufficient merit to take upon himself the sins of the people, who give him alms as their privilege, not as a charity.

Lady Lawley describes him as being on a pilgrimage from Benares to Rameswaram. "He refused to sit down while I kept him waiting, preferring to stand in the broiling sun till I was ready. He was under a vow not to sit down from sunrise till sunset. His hair was matted with grease and dirt, and it trailed on the ground when it was not hung across his arm. I put out my hand to touch it, but he started back with a look of terror lest he should lose merit by contact with a foreigner. Nor would he consent to take a rupee from my hand. I threw it on the ground at his feet and he picked it up."

Hindu will still bestow alms on the ascetic. To allow him to suffer hunger or thirst would bring a curse upon the whole neighbourhood. In defence the people feed him and see that he wants for nothing. In return he blesses them, controls the evil spirits so that they shall not plague them, gives them charms to cure disease and to keep away bad dreams and all kinds of ill-luck.

The Sadhu in the sketch has allowed his hair to grow in fulfilment of a vow made by his mother that it should never be cut. If he did not twist the long matted strand over his arm it would trail upon the ground. Another vow that he made was never to sit down to rest between sunrise and sunset. The marvel is that he consented to stand before the artist and permit his portrait to be taken. Probably he did not understand what the English lady was about. He may have thought that she, like the Hindus, desired to benefit by the huge store of merit that he had acquired in the performance of his strange vows, and that this was her method of drawing some of it upon herself.

The belief of the people in the sanctity of the ascetic seems childish and harmless; but sometimes it is neither the one nor the other. The belief is that every action of the Sadhu is sacred, that he cannot sin; and that in assisting him to fulfil any human desire a highly meritorious act is performed and a blessing obtained. This superstition opens the door to the performance of various immoral actions in the name of religion.

There are several degrees of sanctity among Hindu ascetics, who may all be classed under the term of Sadhu. The highest form of asceticism is the Hindu practice of Yoga. It is not confined to any caste or tribe; the Yogi is usually a man who desires to give up the world and attain union with his deity. His method is intense concentration of thought assisted by fixing the eyes on some given point; or it may be accomplished by postures. He usually repeats the name of the deity or a muntram. The object of contemplation is frequently the tip of the nose, which causes him to squint. He also regulates his breathing. The result is self-hypnotism and trance, during which he is believed to be in direct communication with the deity.

Under the influence of the trance he claims to be able to attain the art of levitation, clairvoyancy, clairaudiency, and prophecy. He believes that he can make himself invisible, traverse space, animate the dead, and obtain command over material matter. Naturally the human being who is credited with the possession of supernatural powers of this description is greatly feared and venerated.

The true Yogi is not often seen in South India; but there are many ascetics who have dabbled in Yoga, and claim powers which they take care shall not be put to a test. It is impossible to say how much these people rely on trickery to obtain their results; but it is certain that they assume a bold front and leave the oriental imagination to do a great deal for them.

The Sanyâsi by the practice of some of the Yoga ceremonies attains a certain degree of sanctity. He may become a Yogi if he chooses to persevere. He resides where he pleases, or wanders at will with his disciple, who serves also as an attendant, and is a link between himself and the world. He may stay for some weeks or months at a temple and be a great attraction to the worshippers; but this does not mean that he serves the temple or takes part in the ritual usually performed by the purohits.

A lower class of ascetic known in the south is the Valluvan or village astrologer, usually a rogue and a charlatan with sufficient cunning to impose upon the most ignorant of the villagers. He constitutes himself pujari to the tree devil, and manages to make a living in one way or another out of the credulity of the people.

The Yogi, Sanyâsi, and Valluvan are sometimes erroneously called Fakirs. A Fakir is a Muhammadan ascetic. The term Faqih is Arabic for theologian. The Faqiha or theologians learned the Quran by heart with many of the Commentaries and Traditions. They passed on their knowledge to their scholars and their disciples in the old days. At the present time the Faqihas are as a rule men whose only claim to learning is the power to repeat the Quran like a parrot.

The Fakir may come under the name of Sadhu; but he cannot be called a Yogi or a Sanyâsi, any more than a Yogi or Sanyâsi can be called a Fakir.

Dr. Pennell, who worked for years among the tribes on the border in the north, once went to Rishika, a suburb of Hardwar, and the favourite resort of ascetics. He spent a short time there as a Sadhu among Sadhus. He was never mistaken for a Hindu Yogi or a Muhammadan Fakir; but was recognised as a Christian ascetic. He wore a turban and a long white garment, and he begged his way with his disciple. He learned a great deal of the customs of Sadhus while he lived with them.

A LEARNED ASCETIC

He has given up his profession or trade and retired from the world to study the Vedas, the sacred books of the Hindus, and concentrate his thoughts on the Deity.

The curious regard for religion inherited by every oriental ensured his being treated with respect; and he was allowed to practise his asceticism in his own way. Nobody tried to proselytise him. The experience was not pleasant. It was like living in a lunatic asylum where no control or order was enforced. Among the company he recognised a few as genuine enthusiasts; but the majority of his companions he believed to be harmlessly insane. The little sense they might originally have possessed had vanished under the performance of strange austerities. Many of the more ignorant and undoubtedly weak-minded wore no clothing whatever, and their habits were indescribably disgusting.

Yet when any one of these men appeared in a Hindu village, the people welcomed him with delight. They looked upon him as full of merit, and therefore sinless and incapable of sinning. In their eyes he was more divine than human; and was able to confer all kinds of blessings by the mere power of his will. They believed that the dust his foot touched acquired healing power by the contact, and was able in itself to cure disease and nullify the evil ascribed to malignant devils.

If the people credited the power of the Sadhu

to bless, their belief in his power to curse was still stronger. During his stay in the neighbourhood the greatest care was observed not to give offence. Even the Brahman landowner feared to rouse his ill-humour. As for the pariah, he trembled at the very sight of him; and when he brought his offering of money, he had to leave it in the dust some distance away for the ascetic to pick up at his leisure.

The silver coin with which the Sadhu was paid for standing while Lady Lawley painted his picture had to be deposited on the ground; he would not receive it direct from any hand. All through the sitting he was full of anxiety lest he should be defiled by the chance touch of one of the Government House servants.

This fear arose, not because he held them personally in contempt, but because he was afraid that the acquired merit with which he was filled should vanish under desecrating contact with the unholy. Where would he be without that valuable asset which made him feared and welcomed at the same time? It could only be restored by the performance of more austerities, more long pilgrimages, more concentration of thought with the monotonous contemplation of the tip of his nose.

Mad and fanatical as he may be, the Sadhu never altogether loses that fraction of human shrewdness which enables him to understand how his own interests may best be served.

A faint shadow of tradition lingers round that haunt of holy men in Triplicane. It is provokingly bare of detail. In the old days an ancient man of extreme sanctity, with long hair, ash-smeared body and begging-bowl occupied the corner. An Englishman in the service of the Company had occasion to ride past him every morning on his way to office. For some reason known only to the horse the animal shied at the old man, to the discomfort and annoyance of his rider. The Englishman was at first irritated with his horse. Finding correction of no use he transferred his anger from the animal to the man. He ordered him to move. No notice was taken of the command. The Englishman's wrath increased and he called the Sanyâsi an idle beggar and a vagabond. Magicians of all ages have had the reputation of being short in the temper. The old man was roused at last. He stood up and levelled curses at him continuously as long as he remained in sight. The Englishman rode away breathing out threatenings of flogging and jail. Tradition is apt to be a little negligent of detail. It is in this case; for it simply records the fact that for ever afterwards misfortune dogged the steps of the Englishman. How, when, and where his ill-luck overtook him we are not told; but we are assured that he was the most unlucky person that ever set foot on India's coral strand; and he put it all down to his little rencontre with the Sadhu of the Triplicane high road.

THE
MUHAMMADANS OF TRIPLICANE

The Prophet cried with a loud voice: "Trust in God; yet tie the camel's leg."

Jelalu' d-din Rumi.

CHAPTER III

THE MUHAMMADANS OF TRIPLICANE

TRIPLICANE is the Muhammadan quarter of Madras. There also is situated the palace of the Prince of Arcot, a descendant of the Nawabs of the Carnatic. One of his ancestors built the palace at Chepauk, now turned into government offices. The broad street called the Triplicane high road is said to have been widened and improved by the French when they occupied Madras, 1746–49. The street is interesting. Always thronged with people, it has nothing European about it. Carriages and motors roll up and down the Mount road, but they rarely pass through Triplicane town.

The best houses are occupied by Muhammadan merchants. In the smaller dwellings live the poorer classes, also Muslims. The windows are closely shuttered with venetians. Behind those windows, whether they belong to the rich or the poor, lies an unknown backwater, whose surface is never ruffled by the busy outer world. Unless the European has been in actual touch with the inner life of the Muhammadan it is difficult to comprehend its extraordinary limitations.

Whether it be the wife of a rich trader or of a journeyman tailor, she may not pass the threshold of the street door unless she is closely veiled. Her only means of exercise and of breathing fresh air is in the small back-yard with its high walls, excluding every other sight but the blue sky and the tall cocoanut-palm that grows in her neighbour's yard or her own. She lives within the sound of the sea; but her eyes have never rested upon it. The roar of the surf when the monsoon wind blows comes in over that high wall. She may perhaps listen to its deep thunder as the breakers fall in a triple line on the sandy shore. It conveys nothing to her mind and conjures up nothing in her imagination. So narrow is her world that she has no desire to follow up the roar of the waves and fill her eyes with the light and colour of the Indian seas.

From the other side of the house comes the murmur of the noisy street, and she is drawn to the venetianed windows to look down upon the turbans of the Muhammadan men passing by; and on the roofs of the jutkas and bullock-carts in the roadway. The people are all strangers to her and the scene soon grows monotonous. She turns back to her own narrow horizon where the births, deaths and marriages have an absorbing interest.

However secluded her life may be it is not spent in idleness. If she is the wife of a tailor or clerk, she passes long hours embroidering muslin with cheap cotton. She gets very little for it as she is obliged to take what the merchant offers. The money helps to buy a piece of bright-coloured satin, which is made up into a pair of pyjamas for her little girl, such as the child wears who is seated on a chair.

If she is the wife of a rich merchant nothing will induce her to touch a needle. In India there is no honour in labour; and it is an understood thing that only those who are obliged do manual work. The merchant's wife has no obligation to earn, and she is able to live in idleness; not a dreamy somnolent idleness by any means, but an unprofitable life of gossip, intrigue, squabble and self-indulgence. Her time is fully employed, although her long fingers never touch needle or book.

The most interesting event in a Muslim woman's life whatever her condition may be is marriage, her own or a relative's. Next in interest is a birth or death; but neither of these has as many ceremonies connected with it as marriage.

The daily round—the preparation of food, the treatment of ailments, the observation of omens, and the lengthy toilet—fills the day. She does not ask for anything different. Born and brought up to it, she has no wish to alter her circumstances. The cry is raised outside the harem for emancipation, for a lifting of the curtain; but it finds little echo in the heart of the gosha woman. To bring her out without a very gradual preparation would upset all her ideas of propriety; would outrage her sense of decency. The disgrace of liberty would outweigh any pleasure that she might feel on seeing the outside world. After the ultra-retired life she would be confused and at a complete loss to know how to behave in public.

Worse still would be the attitude of the outer world towards her. The Muhammadan has no time-honoured public opinion founded on chivalry, such as underlies European society, to guide him in his conduct towards women. He would show his disapproval of her appearance unveiled by adopting a rude rough manner, such as the lower class of European would exhibit in his behaviour towards one of his own women who had put on masculine dress. It is the mark of respectability to be gosha, and it is the ambition of every Muhammadan woman to attain to it. The wife of the head gardener at Government House, Ootacamund, a man who was neither rich nor in a high position, admitted that she had never seen the garden where her husband had worked for many years, although she had lived close to it all her life, so great was her fear of breaking her gosha and thus "losing caste" in the eyes of her neighbours.

The Muhammadans marry young, but not as young as the Hindus. The man is usually eighteen before he is given a wife; the girl is about fourteen. The bride and bridegroom are not consulted in the choice which is made for them by their parents. As a rule, they do not see each other till the day when they begin their honeymoon. Up to that time they have to take each other on faith. They listen on both sides to glowing descriptions overdrawn and exaggerated, and are assured again and again that Allah has been good, and that each has won a prize in the lottery of marriage. The girl longs for youth; the man for beauty—he is sure of youth and need not trouble himself on that score. How often bitter disappointment enters their lives can only be conjectured. The harem knows how to keep its secrets.

Since the young people are not allowed to choose for themselves, there must of necessity be a third person to bring them together. This is usually an old woman of the lower and poorer class who follows the trade of pedlar. She is a privileged person, a link between the outer world and the harem, and she is warmly welcomed by the gosha women. In addition to bringing her wares for sale, she is the purveyor of gossip of all kinds. The purchase of her goods—the only form of shopping permitted—is never hurried over. She is quite content to sit and wait while her treasures are fingered and examined, and often discussed with more depreciation than praise. She understands exactly what it all means, and that the article most criticised is the article most desired.

She looks on good-naturedly, munches the sweets that are offered, and occupies the time in

MUHAMMADAN CHILD OF NOBLE BIRTH
IN GOLD EMBROIDERED COAT

Round the neck are several handsome jewelled necklaces.

relating all that she has seen and heard since her last visit. It is of a personal nature and well spiced with scandal. She narrates how the master-tailor living in Royapettah, and employing no less than twenty dhirzees, beat his wife two days ago. She had neglected to see to the preparation of the chicken pillao. The cashmere cloth merchant had lost his son in a railway accident up north. The hakeem's child was ill of a strange complaint, supposed to have been caused by the evil eye of a Hindu widow, who stopped in the road where he was playing to watch him. Cassim, employed in the post office, was taking another wife. Did any one ever hear of such folly? He had one already, and he a poor man! It was only the well-to-do who could afford to have more than one wife.

Then she comments on the son of a calico merchant who reached his eighteenth birthday some months ago and was not yet married. His mother was looking round for a suitable wife; but these were expensive times, and it was difficult to find a family prepared to be generous in the matter of jewels.

Leaving this bit of news to soak in, she lets her eyes rest on the thirteen-year-old daughter of the house, who is losing her heart to a string of imitation pearls in the old woman's basket. A little later she puts leading questions as to the betrothal of the girl. She manages the business so well that before long she is asked to call on the boy's mother and speak of the girl.

Several visits are paid with long palavers, and at length a definite desire is expressed on both sides that the two young people shall be married. Before even an engagement can be made there is much to be done. The first step is the casting of the horoscopes. For this purpose the services of an astrologer and a mullah are needed. If the elements that dominate the respective horoscopes are favourable, the ceremonies may be proceeded with. If, however, the elements are antagonistic, such as fire in the man's and water in the woman's horoscope, the match must be broken off, as the union would be disastrous.

Allowing that the astrologer has declared that the stars are propitious, and that the mullah has assured them that Allah will regard the union with favour, enquiries have to be made into the pedigree of the families, their connections, and the religious ritual followed by the bridegroom. Then the services of a seer are employed to pronounce upon the omens and give advice as to whether the matter should go any further. And if he says that all is well, preparations are made for a formal betrothal.

Meanwhile the little bride takes no part in these preliminaries. Probably she knows nothing about them. Certainly she is not asked if she approves or is pleased with her parents' designs. She runs free within her father's harem, dressed in brilliant satins and white embroidered muslin, more interested in the games of childhood than in the duties of womanhood. She finds a vague excitement in the glances of her elders, which are more often directed towards her than hitherto; but if she seriously considers the future it is with fear rather than with pleasure. Yet there is never a thought of rebellion against her fate. What is written on her forehead will come to pass whether it brings pain and suffering or joy and pleasure.

A DHURZI OR TAILOR; A MUHAMMADAN

Unless he is extremely poor his wife lives "gosha," *i.e.* in strict seclusion. She embroiders muslin for which she receives very little.

MUHAMMADAN MARRIAGE

Moses heard a shepherd praying thus:

"O God! show me where Thou art that I may become Thy servant, clean Thy shoes, dress Thy hair and fetch Thee milk."

Moses rebuked the man for his foolish prayer. He was ashamed and ran away. God then rebuked Moses, saying:

"To each race I give different ways of praising Me. It is not the words I care for, but the spirit in which they are said. Various are the ways of devotion; but if genuine all are accepted."

The Masnawi (translated by WHINFIELD).

CHAPTER IV

MUHAMMADAN MARRIAGE

MARRIAGE with the Muhammadans is purely civil. From beginning to end religion plays no part in it, although the mullah may be called in. It is the qazi and not the mullah whose assistance is required in making the contract when the time comes. Before the magistrate is summoned, however, there are many ceremonies to be performed. Every little incident is taken advantage of by the inmates of the harem, to whom all domestic functions are very precious excuses for excitement and social gatherings.

After the astrologer and the seer have been consulted and enquiry has been made concerning the sectarianism of the families, the pedigree and the general health of the young people is reported on, the dowry of the bride and the income of the bridegroom are arranged, and a formal exchange of betel-leaves and areca-nut takes place. Nothing is put on paper, but each side has witnesses, and the betrothal is finally accomplished.

It is followed by a number of entertainments. Their character depends entirely upon the circumstances of the parents. If rich, they are lavish and magnificent and may last many weeks. If the people are poor, they may consist of only two or three social gatherings in a humble way. Friends and relatives are entertained with food and sweetmeats, sherbet and fruit. Musicians and dancing girls are hired, and at night a display of fireworks is given. Every little incident is made the occasion of one of these gatherings, even down to taking the measurement of the bride and bridegroom for their wedding dresses.

As the preparation for these social functions is carried out by the women, it is easy to understand their delight in a marriage and all that it brings in its train. Neither a birth nor a death entails as much feasting and entertaining.

When at last the preliminary festivities are at an end—not because they are by any means exhausted, but from failure of the purse to sustain any more charges upon it—the qazi is sent for. He is a magistrate, a man of birth and education, as may be seen by a glance at his picture. His

A KHAZI (QAZI), MUHAMMADAN MAGISTRATE

Besides other offices he performs marriages. He is usually a man of good birth and is highly respected.

bearing is courteous and full of dignity, especially if he be of Arab descent. His features are Semitic and his complexion of a pale olive.

A Muhammadan is allowed by the Quran to have four wives. Unless he is a rich man, he rarely burdens himself with that number, as each wife is supposed to have a separate suite of rooms and her own servants. One or two at most suffice for the Muslims of Triplicane, as a rule. Whatever the number and whatever the order in which they are married, the bride who is chosen by the man's mother is considered the chief wife. The marriage is called the shahdi, and the ceremonies connected with it, in which the bridegroom's mother takes part, are never repeated. The other marriages are made less formally. One is called the nikah, and the other the murta. The latter may be made by a declaration before witnesses of the man's intention and the woman's consent. The object of these easily formed alliances is to prevent the birth of illegitimate children, and to give the offspring of temporary unions a legal claim upon their father.

The qazi comes to the bridegroom's house dressed in richly embroidered robes. In old days he was carried in a smart palankeen, but in these times he is more likely to arrive by motor-car. He is received with honour, and immediately the bride's mother is sent for. Closely veiled, she comes in a covered conveyance, and on her appearance the legal ceremony that makes the actual marriage begins.

But where is the bride? Surely she is necessary at this point of the proceedings! She is left behind in her father's harem and has no voice in the matter.

The mother has her lawyer or vakil with her, and the business begins as the tomtoms and pipes are hushed and the company silenced for a time. The dowry is mentioned and formally promised before the qazi. The bridegroom perhaps is asked to make a confession of faith. Then he joins hands with the vakil in ratification of the contract. The mother gives her consent and the marriage is concluded. The qazi departs with a ceremonious leave-taking, and the wedding party adjourns to the bride's house.

For the first time bride and bridegroom are to meet. The mothers and sisters of both are present with other relatives. Musicians with pipes and drums are assembled in the verandahs and yard, and dancing women chant their love songs. Even now, though they are husband and wife, their meeting is restricted and they are not allowed to see each other. A curtain is placed between them and they are seated on either side. The bridegroom tosses flowers and jewels to his bride over the curtain; and there is plenty of fun and laughter and joking, not of the most refined character. Flower petals and raw rice are thrown over the couple to bring them good luck and fertility.

The evening approaches. It is time for the bride to be taken to the home her husband has prepared for her. Closely veiled, she is escorted to the house by her relatives and is left in the room that is to be hers for the future. Impatiently her husband enters and approaches his bride. Lifting her veil, he gazes on the drooping head and downcast face for the first time. Whether she be "as beautiful as the moon" or as ugly as a village herdswoman, he is bound to her for life, or until he chooses to divorce her.

After marriage the next event of importance is the birth of the child. Happy for the mother if it is a son! and miserable is the woman to whom the blessing is denied. Children in the harem form the one bright spot in the gosha life. They are not confined within the walls like their elders, but are allowed to stray out into the sunshine. It is only later that the girl is caught and forbidden to pass the threshold, while the boy goes free.

It has been said that there are no children in India; they are either infants or they are grown-up men and women as far as their minds are concerned. The entire absence of reserve in the conversations carried on before them by their elders informs them of many things that are scrupulously kept from the ears of a British child. This precocious knowledge does not cloud their young minds. It may destroy their innocence to a certain degree, but youth remains with its spontaneous joyousness; and there is no prettier sight in the East than the round-faced mite of six or seven years old with her soft shy eyes and delicate skin.

Like the children of other countries, the little ones have their games. Those who have read *Behind the Bungalow*, by E. H. A., will remember the pathetic story of the butler's little son who played his solemn games in the dust and made marvellous feasts for imaginary guests. Whether it is the effect of the hot climate or of constitutional inertia, the inheritance of a lethargic nation, the Indian child inclines to less boisterous play than the children of colder countries. An English

A MUHAMMADAN GIRL

boy loves nothing better than to personate the pirate, or the hunter of fabulously savage wild beasts. With his stick held as a rifle he shoots down his enemies and carries off prisoners and booty. This kind of thing does not appeal to the boy of the East, whose preference runs to making feasts, to entertaining his friends as a rajah and riding in state, or to playing the merchant and overreaching his customers in bargaining.

The Oriental girl loves nothing so much as a marriage. If she is the fortunate possessor of a doll, it becomes in time very much wedded to various spouses, chiefly sticks and stones. The old women in the harem are always ready to join in this game. Often real entertainments are made with sweets and sherbet, musicians and dancing women hired for the occasion. Various members of the harem personate the different characters, for which there is the fun of dressing up. The festivities extend over several days if the family is well-off; and there is almost as much excitement over it as if the whole thing were real.

The dolls of the Muhammadan children have no features and are little more than mere bundles of rags rolled up. It is due to a belief among Muslims that any figure made by the hand of man will receive life at the last day, and will reproach its maker for having brought it into existence without having the power to endow it with human and spiritual privileges.

A tradition relates that Ayesha, the favourite wife of the Prophet, purchased a carpet with a pattern in which figures were represented. She laid it down for her husband to rest upon when he returned home. As he entered the doorway and his eyes fell upon the new acquisition, he stopped short and looked at it with displeasure. Ayesha was much troubled.

"Oh, Messenger of God! I repent to God and his Messenger!" she cried. "What fault have I committed that you do not enter?"

"What is this carpet?" Muhammad asked.

"I have bought it for you to sit and rest upon," replied Ayesha.

"Verily the maker of pictures will be punished on the day of resurrection," he answered, "when God will desire him to bring them to life. A house which contains pictures is not visited by the angels."

In another tradition the Prophet classes all artists with murderers and parricides. It is on account of this condemnation that the drawings of Muhammadan artists are usually in floral designs

DAUGHTER OF MEANJEE SAIT, A RICH MUHAMMADAN MERCHANT

Her ankles are loaded with heavy silver bangles. The red voluminous cloth is a gold-bordered veil capable of completely shrouding her face and figure.

and arabesques. They are extremely beautiful, and exceed in delicacy of detail the work of Hindu artists. In no place is this so remarkable as in the design of the Taj Mahal. Its decorations as well as its architecture are incomparable. They set the visitor wondering what might have been produced if the architect, sculptor, and artist had been allowed a free hand.

When British rupees were first circulated in India the figure of the sovereign in relief was regarded with distrust. Fortunately for the peace of the merchant, the eye was so small as to be almost invisible. Through this loophole the followers of the Prophet found a way of escape from the difficulty, deciding that no harm would come in the use of the money.

The Prophet forbade innovation of all kinds. He was to be blindly followed without deviation. A Muhammadan of South India who suggested the substitution of Hindustani for Arabic in a certain prayer was excommunicated publicly in the principal mosque in Madras. This close adherence to a dogmatic system is inimical to progress. Instead of welcoming new forms of truth, new sciences, new ideas, the orthodox Muhammadan turns from them with suspicion and distrust.

THE FAITH OF ISLAM

O *Pardoning God!* I cry to Thee
Thy pardon to implore;
O *Sovereign Lord!* subdue through me
Who e'er subverts Thy law.

Thy glory, *Glorious Being!* doth
My feeble strength increase;
O *Thou who humblest in the dust!*
Cause lying tongues to cease.

Knowledge and understanding give,
O *Giver of All!* to me;
Sustainer! for my sustenance
I look for ease from Thee.

The souls of all Thy enemies,
O *Seizer of spirits!* seize;
O *Scatterer of gifts!* increase desire
In beauty's devotees.

O *Humbler!* humble Thou the power
Of all who Thee oppose;
O *Thou Who raiseth!* raise me up
In spite of these my foes.

(Translation of a poem on the names of Allah.)

CHAPTER V

THE FAITH OF ISLAM

VAGUE ideas concerning the faith of Muhammadans exist in the minds of those who have not studied the religions of the East. Living side by side with the Hindus, the Muslim sometimes gets the credit of being an idolater. Those who know that he follows the teaching of a book of scripture called the Quran, and reveres a Prophet named Muhammad, are nevertheless sometimes ignorant of the fact that the Muhammadan, the Jew, and the Christian all believe in the broad historical outline of the Old Testament; and acknowledge the Patriarchs and Moses, the legend of Adam and Eve, their life in the Garden of Eden, and their fall.

The interpretation of the Old Testament by the teachers of the three creeds varies considerably. The Christian accuses the exponents of Muhammad's doctrines of overlaying the simple tale of the Patriarchs with tradition for which there is no historical foundation. The Muhammadans, on the other hand, complain that the Christians have perverted the truth and shorn sacred history of all its details. However much they may differ in this respect, the general acceptance of the outlines by all three should create a sympathy between them which could not exist between the heathen and any one of the believers in the Old Testament Scriptures.

Muhammad was born to a degenerate faith into which gross error had crept. His spirit revolted against the error and he rose as a reformer, calling for a drastic reformation. His preachings drew a large following, and he was made a leader; his sayings and writings were collected in a book. The book received the name of the Quran. It was believed that Muhammad wrote it at the dictation of the angel Gabriel, who brought the message direct from God. Rules were laid down for the conduct of the individual as well as for the community. They related to prayer, fasting, ablutions, cleanliness, diet, and other matters connected with the daily life. Moses gave the same kind of rules to the Israelites. In these days some of them would be called the practice of eugenics rather than religious observances.

The Quran is highly venerated; and the followers of the Prophet learn it by heart. Some of the religious exercises consist of a repetition of its words. Sentences must be said over and over again, the greatest care being taken to pronounce every syllable correctly. As to the interpretation of the Quran, the Muhammadan is not asked to think for himself. He is to follow example and precept blindly, as others have followed before him.

One of the earliest disciples of the Prophet was observed to ride his camel several times round a rock. He was asked why he did so. He replied that he did not know; he had seen the Prophet do it and was following his example. His conduct met with approval and commendation. He was exhibiting in his action a faith worthy of imitation; it was placed on record, that it might be a lesson to those who should come after.

There are five acts that are called the five pillars of Islam. They should be performed by all good Muhammadans. They are the confession of faith; the periods of prayer; the fast of Ramazan; the giving of prescribed alms; the pilgrimage to Mecca. In addition to these there is circumcision, purification, obedience to parents, etc.

What a Muhammadan may not do is to eat forbidden food or act in any way contrary to the directions of the Quran and the Traditions. When he is in doubt, he is to abstain from the contemplated deed.

The part of the Muhammadan's life that impresses the stranger most is his obedience to the call of prayer. If he is within hearing of the cry of the Muezzin, he goes to the mosque, puts off his shoes, and prostrates himself within the building. If, however, he happens to be working, travelling, or amusing himself where no mosque is at hand, he stops as the sun nears the horizon, spreads his carpet and says his prayers, indifferent to what the world may think or say.

Three or five periods are observed for prayer. The three are sunrise, sunset, and night. The odd numbers are curious. The Muslim believes that the Deity loves odd numbers. "God is odd; He loves the odd," said a Tradition. The Muhammadan is careful to use odd numbers on every occasion; in the repetition of his prayers, in the date that he chooses for starting on a journey or for beginning a work, and in every other matter wherein a number enters, he shows his preference for the odd figure.

SYED SHAH FAKHRUD-DEEN SUF, A MUHAMMADAN MUNSHI

He declares he taught Lord Roberts Hindustani and still corresponds with him.

The service at the mosque—the first pillar of Islam—consists of the confession of faith which is made after the Muezzin has called several times upon the name of God.

Muezzin. "Allahu Akbar!" (God is great!).

Worshippers. "Allahu Akbar!"

Muezzin. "I confess that there is no God but God!"

Worshippers. "I confess that there is no God but God!"

Muezzin. "I confess that Muhammad is the apostle of God!"

Worshippers. "I confess that Muhammad is the apostle of God!"

Muezzin. "Come to prayer!"

Worshippers. "I have no power or strength but from God most High and Great."

Muezzin. "Come to do good!"

Worshippers. "What God wills will be; what He wills not will not be."

Other supplications may follow in public or private. The worshipper must be careful to kneel and stand correctly with the hands and the feet in the proper position. The eyes must be fixed on the spot which will be touched at the end of the prayer by the forehead in prostration.

The observance of the periods of prayer—viz. sunrise, sunset, and night—form the second pillar of Islam.

The character of nearly all Muhammadan prayer

is praise and propitiation. Mercies are also asked for, and supplications made for pity and for preservation from evil. The following is one of their prayers. Others are similar but longer.

"O God, our Lord! Give us the blessing of this life, and also the blessings of life everlasting. Save us from the torments of hell."

The prayers are said in Arabic and there is constant repetition. It follows that they become mechanical and lose their spiritual effect. As a writer has observed, the Muhammadan faith is pre-eminently the creed of the soldier and worker, the religion of the individual who has no leisure to think. It is not suitable for one who longs to find a solution for the problems presented by the sin and suffering of the world.

Muhammadans have no caste, no peerage, no class divisions. The only divisions that exist, and some of these are strongly marked, are sectarian in nature. They accept no leader but they acknowledge the head of a tribe or the head of a family. War is only undertaken in the name of religion; and for this reason alone will Muhammadans combine. The leader must be sent specially by God.

The Indian Muhammadans have been brought

under British rule and have been taught to acknowledge the authority of the King-Emperor. They have learned, moreover, that the British rule is beneficial to the community and brings peace. Though they submit to a temporal power politically, they would not tolerate for a moment any interference with their traditional ceremonies, religious, social, or domestic. These were received direct from the Prophet, and have been preserved in a spirit of conservatism that has no equal in the history of the world.

The third pillar of Islam is the fast of Ramazan. It lasts thirty days. During that time the faithful must not eat or drink between the hours of sunrise and sunset. In a hot climate like Madras it must be very trying. The rich man who is not obliged to labour turns night into day as far as he is able, and so eludes the difficulty; but the tradesman and mechanic cannot afford to do this. It is wonderful how the poorer classes of Triplicane maintain their fast; yet they do it honestly, making up for lost time by drinking and eating largely immediately after sunset and just before sunrise.

The fourth pillar of Faith is a ceremonious and systematic almsgiving. Canon Sell, in his admirable book, *The Faith of Islam*, says: "In India the payment is left to each person's conscience. Whilst there is not much regularity in the payment, due credit must be given for the care which Musalmans take of their poor." This care of the poor is not peculiar to the Muhammadans. The Hindus also charge themselves with the support of their own poor. Each family looks after its relations and no one need beg. Some prefer to join the profession of begging for various reasons, but the unwritten law compels the able-bodied of a family to look after the disabled.

The Muhammadans have several festivals. One of the most striking is the Muharram, if it can be termed a festival. It is called after the name of the first month in the Muslim year. It is a commemorative ceremony during which the people mourn for the death of Ali, the Prophet's son-in-law, and Husain and Hasan, the Prophet's grandsons.

Ali was the fourth Khalif in succession to Muhammad. He had received instruction orally from the Prophet himself; and he followed closely in the steps of the great teacher.

By this time the Muhammadans were divided, and Ali had a rival in the person of Muavia, who caused his assassination. The followers of Ali raised his son Hasan to the khalifate. Hasan was poisoned by his perfidious wife, and Muavia succeeded him. After Muavia's death his son Yezid occupied the khalifate. He was a man of bad character and the people soon tired of him and his debaucheries. A message was sent to Husain asking him to assume the khalifate.

Without waiting to discover what support he might rely upon, he responded to the call, and went to Kufa, whence the summons came. He took with him a small escort of mounted men and foot soldiers. He was met by three thousand men who opposed his entry into Kufa. They outnumbered his own troops by more than ten to one, and he at once recognised the impossibility of conquering them. He turned to his followers and gave them permission to leave him and to join his opponents. They refused with the remarkable words: "Oh! son of the Apostle of God! what excuse could we give to thy grandfather on the day of resurrection, if we abandoned thee to the hands of thine enemies?"

They were attacked and fell after fierce fighting until only Husain and his infant son were left. The grandson of the Prophet seated himself by the river Euphrates to drink. There was a pause.

No one dared to turn his bow against the sacred person of a descendant of Muhammad. An arrow, shot at a venture, pierced the ear of the little boy and killed him. His sorrowing father laid the body down. Then, being oppressed with thirst, he stooped to drink. As he did so a flight of arrows was discharged and he was wounded. He rose to his feet and fought bravely, but fell at last and died.

His death caused a lasting division among the followers of the Prophet which has never been healed. The two factions are known as the Sunnis and Shiahs. The days of mourning observed by the Shiahs keep alive the feud. The quarrel began on political grounds; but distinct religious differences have since arisen which need not be followed here.

Triplicane is full of Shiahs who mourn for Ali and his two sons. It seems at the time as if the assassinations had occurred only the week before instead of more than a thousand years ago. Lady Lawley was able, through the good offices of a friend, to see the procession of the tabut or shrine as it was carried along the Triplicane high road to be cast into a tank. The exhibition of grief is in the beating of the breast, the swaying of the body, and the cries of "Ali! Noble Husain! Noble Husain!" The excitement grows. The men weep real tears —the tear lies very near the surface in the East— and they show every appearance of being distracted by grief. The sight is impressive as well as picturesque; but the looker-on knows all the time that the emotion is assumed at will and is not spontaneous.

In commemoration of the deaths the Muhammadans make models of the tombs of their departed heroes and carry them in procession. They are called tabuts or taziahs, and are of various shapes and sizes, gaily ornamented with tinsel and colour. Inside is sometimes placed an object that represents the property that once belonged to Ali or his sons —a turban, a shield, a sword, or bow and arrows.

The tabut rests in a hall or temporary shelter made of bamboo and palm leaves. Decorated poles or standards are ranged against the walls of the hall. Some of the standards have the figure of a hand on the top, emblematic of the five members of the Prophet's family. Others have a lime representing the head of Husain as it was carried on a spear. During the Muharram the people assemble every evening in the hall and seat themselves on the ground round the tabut. The sad story of Husain is chanted, and when the singers pause for breath the company breaks into a chorus of lamentation.

Only men and boys attend these gatherings. The women remain in the harem. The story is told to them there, and they echo the lamentations that they hear outside. All alike are filled with a strange emotional excitement which has a peculiar fascination for the impressionable Oriental. It does not appeal, however, to the practical European, who sees in it only the picturesque. The colour and noise, the glittering tinsel of the tabuts, and the chanting of the story make it a scene never to be forgotten. The procession has passed along the road for centuries without a break and with an unchanging ritual. It will continue to pass each year as long as a beneficent Government protects the religious liberties of its Muhammadan subjects. Many were the riots that these processions caused before the reign of law and order was established by the British.

At the end of the commemoration the tabuts are taken away from the halls and cast into some tank or piece of water. In carrying them to their destination the Muhammadans sometimes have to pass a Hindu temple. The presence of Muslims

A MUHAMMADAN OFFICER OF THE ARAB GUARD OF HIS HIGHNESS THE NIZAM OF HYDERABAD

in Hindu quarters, even though they are only passers-by, stirs up the race hatred that is always smouldering between the two nations, and expressions of animosity are provoked on both sides. It takes very little to fire such inflammable material; and in the old days free fights were common occurrences. The authorities, in the interests of peace, were obliged to forbid Muhammadan processions to pass through streets in which temples stood; and Hindu processions were equally forbidden to pass mosques. The obligation continues and the laws are in no way relaxed; otherwise we should have an exchange of amenities, as the humorists put it, between the two nations in the present day, in the shape of pig-killing in the mosques and cow-killing in the temples.

The Hindu temple in the Vellore Fort was desecrated by the killing of a sacred bull in the devasthanum. It was in consequence deserted; and for many years it remained open to the bats and jackals and to the foot of the stranger. On account of the expense entailed in the removal of the desecration by ceremonies and almsgiving, its restoration was not undertaken. But the Government repaired it and prevented it from falling into ruin; and it is kept as an ancient monument of great historical interest.

Sometimes a disturbance is created among the Muhammadans themselves. The Sunnis take umbrage at the abuse showered upon their historical leaders by the Shiahs, and a breach of the peace follows; but as the head men are made responsible for the conduct of their co-religionists, the hot-headed young men are restrained by their elders.

It is curious to note how the religion and customs of the conquered affect the conquerors where annihilation has not been carried out. Canon Sell says that Indian Musalmans have copied in their feasts many Hindu ceremonies. The procession of the tazias or tabuts, and the casting of them into the water is very similar to the procession at the Hindu feast of the Durga puja, known in South India as the Dussara. The image of Durga, the wife of Siva, is thrown into the Ganges. The fact was that the Muhammadan form of worship was too simple for a country in which an allegorical and idolatrous religion predominated, appealing to the senses and the imagination rather than to the understanding and the heart; consequently Muhammadan festivals have borrowed from it a variety of pagan rites and a pompous and gorgeous ceremonial. While this has done much to add to the superstition of the Musalmans in India, it has possibly softened their intolerant spirit. Certain it is that the Shiahs and Sunnis of Triplicane have learned to live side by side in peace.

MUHAMMADAN FESTIVALS AND SUPERSTITIONS

Prayer carries us half way to God; fasting brings us to the door of His palace; almsgiving procures us admission.

Saying of the Khalif Abd'-ul-Aziz.

CHAPTER VI

MUHAMMADAN FESTIVALS AND SUPERSTITIONS

The three Muhammadan festivals which come under the notice of the Europeans are the Ramazan, the Muharram, and the Buqr'Id (Buckreed). The first, the Ramazan, is a fast. The second, the Muharram, is a memorial function to commemorate a death. The third is a feast, and the most important of all the feasts properly so called. It is the feast of sacrifice.

The Buqr'Id commemorates the sacrifice of Ishmael. The Muhammadans believe that Abraham was ordered by God to offer up Ishmael, the son of Hagar. He proceeded to carry out the divine command, but was unable to cut his son's throat.

"It is through pity and compassion for me that you allow the knife to miss," said Ishmael. "Blindfold yourself and then sacrifice me."

Abraham followed his directions, drew the knife

as he thought across the throat of his son. When he removed the bandage from his eyes he found that the angel Gabriel had substituted a sheep for the boy.

The chief feature of the feast is the sacrifice of blood. An animal, usually a goat, must be killed by the head of each household in the name of God. Its flesh is cooked and eaten and part of it is given to the poor. The festival is made the occasion of a holiday. The Muhammadans dress in their smartest garments; and pay friendly visits, when sweetmeats are eaten and much sherbet is drunk.

Similar festivities accompany lesser festivals observed every year. One of these feasts is called the festival of the seven blessings or Salams.

I. Peace shall be the word on the part of a merciful Lord.
II. Peace be on Noah throughout the worlds.
III. Peace be on Abraham.
IV. Peace be on Moses and Aaron.
V. Peace be on Elias.
VI. Peace be on you; ye have been good; enter into Paradise.
VII. It is peace till the breaking of the morn.

These seven sentences are written on a mango-leaf or a plantain-leaf by a mullah. While the

A MUHAMMADAN LADY

The headdress is of jasmin blossom. Into the long plait of hair strings of seed pearls are woven. The veil thrown over her shoulders is of silk and gold gauze. The coloured coat is a garment for outdoor wear when taking a drive or paying a visit.

writing is still wet it is washed off with water or milk and the mixture is swallowed; by which means the Muhammadans believe that they can ensure the possession of peace and happiness for the rest of the year. Hindus as well as Muhammadans follow the same ritual in making charms against evil spirits and bad luck. The charm is written on a leaf or a china plate, washed off and swallowed by the subject.

The evil spirits of Islam are jinns or shytans, supernatural beings created out of fire. They are supposed to eat and drink and propagate their species. Some are good and believe in the Prophet; but a great number are said to be of a malicious nature and infidels, who will share hell with unbelieving human beings. The Muhammadans also believe in angels, who, they say, form nine-tenths of creation. They all have their several duties to perform in Heaven and earth. They are invisible to human beings but can be seen by animals. The cock crows when he sees an angel; but when the ass brays they say that he sees a devil, a shytan.

The belief that God has appointed four angels to watch over every man that is born is in accordance with the Christian belief in guardian angels.

There are many variations of the old saying in England: "Four angels round my bed; Two at my feet and two at my head." With the Muslim it is believed that two watch over him by day and two by night, and they remain with him till he dies, whatever may be his conduct.

There are four archangels: *Gabriel*, the chief of God's messengers, who stands nearest the throne of Heaven; *Israfel*, in charge of the trumpet which shall sound the last call; he holds it ready at his lips; at the first blast all life will be destroyed, at the second life will be restored; *Israel*, who receives the souls of men when they die; and *Michael*, who is charged with the sustenance of created beings.

The Muhammadans believe in two fallen angels, named Harut and Marut, who teach sorcery to mankind. Their fall was not occasioned by opposition to the divine power, but through over-confidence in their own power of resisting evil. It was in the time of Enoch, when the wickedness of man was great. The angels, observing it, said to the Lord:

"O Lord! Adam and his descendants whom Thou hast appointed as Thy vice-regents on earth act disobediently."

"If I were to send you on earth, and to give

you lustful and angry dispositions, you too would sin," replied the Lord.

The angels ventured to believe that it would be otherwise; God thereupon gave them permission to select two angels to be sent on earth among men with human passions. Harut and Marut were chosen for their piety. Then God said:

"All day go to and fro on the earth; put an end to the quarrels of men; ascribe no equal to Me; do not commit adultery; drink no wine; and every night repeat the exalted Name of God and by the power of that Name return to Heaven."

For some time they obeyed the divine command; but one day they met a beautiful woman named Zuhra, and through her they fell. She tempted them to drink wine. One said:

"God has forbidden it."

"God is merciful and forgiving," replied the other, and they drank. Under the influence of the wine they killed the husband of Zuhra and revealed to her the "exalted Name." No sooner had they uttered it than it escaped their memory and they were unable to return to Heaven. God punished them, and they were banished for ever from His presence. The woman was changed to the evening star, Venus, and she shines in the sky as a constant warning to men not to presume on their own unaided moral strength; but to fly from temptation.

Many of the Muhammadans in the south of India are undoubtedly of Dravidian extraction. When the Dravidians were conquered by the followers of the Prophet, they were obliged to accept the faith at the point of the sword and be circumcised. They were taught the Quran, and their conquerors were satisfied with its repetition. They did not trouble themselves about the animistic beliefs inherited through many generations from devil-worshipping ancestors. To this day those superstitious beliefs remain in Triplicane; and they are the origin of countless propitiatory ceremonies, the practice of which is purely heathen. This is especially the case among the poorer Muhammadans, the tailors, hawkers, domestic servants, clerks, and shop assistants.

In a curious old book published in Madras early in the nineteenth century, called *Qanun-i-Islam*, directions are given for casting out devils; for controlling "shytans" through whom evil passions may be satisfied; to discover the cause of sickness and cure it; to avert the influence of the evil eye; to prepare love-philtres; to cause enmity between two people; to compass the death of an enemy; to manufacture amulets and charms and to point out lucky and unlucky days.

Magic, black and white, has always had a peculiar fascination for frail humanity. The attraction lies in its presumptuous claim to exercise power over supernatural forces. By white magic benefits that are harmless may be obtained. By black magic every kind of human passion may be satisfied, even though it may bring death and disaster to others. The agents through whom such ends are accomplished are evil spirits. They, like men, will not work for nothing; to gain their assistance worship and propitiation must be employed. The whole cult is of necessity, therefore, blasphemous in its nature. The oriental magician is usually a clever charlatan with a knowledge of the power of suggestion and hypnotism, and a reliance on the ignorance and superstition of the people. Whether Muhammadan or Hindu he makes a living out of his so-called magic without much trouble to himself.

The Muslim magician of South India is consulted before any journey or undertaking is begun. There are lucky and unlucky days, which Herklots in his *Qanum-i-Islam* has given, together with couplets to assist the memory, which he has put into doggerel verse. A traveller starting out on his journey should remember to go:

> East on Saturday and Monday;
> On Friday and Sunday West;
> On Tuesday and Wednesday North;
> On Thursday South addrest.

If the traveller is obliged to go west on Tuesday he will do well to start out from a north door and make such a detour as shall avoid the necessity of facing the west at any time during his journey.

In every month there are seven evil days, when no important work should be begun, no matter how pressing it may be. These are the 3rd, 5th, 13th, 16th, 21st, 24th, and 25th. If the work has already been begun, it may be continued, but the tailor will have no success if he cuts out the dress on one of those dates and touches the material with his scissors for the first time.

The workman is hampered by other considerations besides dates, hours of the day, the waxing or waning of the moon, and the appearance of chance omens. If he is going out on business he has to pay attention to his breakfast. On Saturday, he must eat fish for luck; on Sunday, betel leaf.

On Tuesday he must chew coriander seed. On Wednesday he ought to drink curdled milk, which will bring him health and a fortune. On Thursday he must eat sugar, and he will obtain personal property. On Friday he must take a good breakfast of cooked meats, and his pockets will assuredly be filled with pearls and precious stones.

The best days of the week are Monday, Wednesday, Thursday, and Friday.

The reason for all this care in the choice of days is to be found in the Muhammadan belief in South India in a mythical monster who is always moving round the earth. It is fatal to face him; still more fatal to meet him, even though he is invisible. The seer has to be consulted as to his true position—for a fee, of course—and the traveller starts out or the workman undertakes his task with the assurance that Rijal-ul-gyb, the inimical monster, is looking the other way.

It is not a matter for surprise, therefore, that the dhirzee and the peon should be late, or should fail to appear when they are wanted.

Lucky and unlucky days are not unknown in Europe, or even in up-to-date England. Who is not aware that Friday is said to be unfortunate? There is no need to quote the lines concerning the birth of children or referring to marriage. The doggerel verse about building, buying, and selling are not so familiar:

> Don't build on a Thursday; it's a very bad day;
> For barns built then will be burned, they say.
> Friday and Sat'day are good for nought.
> Folk shouldn't be hired nor new things bought.

Respect for the old saying about turning the beds still lingers at the back of the mind of the modern housemaid. "Turn the beds on Sunday and you will turn your luck away," the luck in the maid's case being connected with a prospective husband.

The housewife must remember that "Maids who come on a Saturday will run away, marry away or stay seven years and a day." If she wants to move she must not forget, "Friday flit; Never sit."

DISEASE, DEVILS, AND DEVIL-DOCTORS

It is said that Heaven has one division more than Hell, to show that God's mercy exceeds His justice.

The Faith of Islam (Sell).

CHAPTER VII

DISEASE, DEVILS, AND DEVIL-DOCTORS

DISEASE among Hindus and Muhammadans is believed to be the direct work of an evil spirit. Idiocy and insanity are possession of the devil, and nothing will persuade the Oriental that it is otherwise. The native doctor must be, first and foremost, something of a magician and be able to cast out devils and control them. The Triplicane Muslims have borrowed part of their ritual from the Hindus, and (like them) use flowers, fruit, sweets, camphor, and butter. They add magic squares and circles, and make their invocations in the name of a jinn or demon coupled with one of the many names of Allah. The invocation is as follows: "I adjure you, Futhoomu Nubeeun, by the seal of Solomon the son of David, come from the east, come from the west, from the right and from the left. In the name of the Deity come. Whatever it be that has taken possession of the body of Cassim here, come out of him! come out of him! come out of him!"

The devil should then depart, and manifest his departure by making the patient scream. The incantation has to be repeated many times, with a sprinkling of ashes or powder and the burning of incense.

The patient is asked questions as to the name of the devil that possesses him, where he came from, and what he is doing there. If the patient will not reply, he is severely flogged; and it is said that the flogging leaves no mark. However that may be, he remembers nothing about it when he returns to his senses.

The exorcist professes, for an additional fee, to catch the devil and put him in a bottle. Needless to say, the bottle is prepared beforehand. A small figure in wax is inserted and the bottle filled with smoke. At the proper moment the smoke is allowed to escape and the figure becomes visible. The operator scores yet another point by threatening to let the devil out upon the company if a further fee is not forthcoming. He assures them that as soon as it is free it will assume gigantic proportions, like the jinn in the Arabian Nights' stories which the fisherman let loose. No one in the audience is bold enough to take the risk, and the magician is paid to carry the devil away and dispose of him safely as he thinks best.

After the evil spirit has been exorcised the patient seems to wake from a bad dream and asks where he is. A prayer is said over him and he is washed and dressed. To prevent a recurrence of the possession an amulet is tied on his arm. It is a magic square written on a piece of palm-leaf or paper. It is folded and enclosed with some relic from the tomb of a pir or saint, a tuft of hair or the bone of some creature, the claw of a leopard or tiger, and the feathers of some particular bird. The whole is sewn in a piece of silk, and it must be worn day and night. With wealthy people these amulets are encased in little cylinders of precious metal; they are tied on the arm above the elbow, or in the case of a woman they may be strung upon her necklace. The preparation of amulets and charms is another source of income to the magician, whether he be Hindu or Muhammadan.

When the Muhammadan hakim is called in, the first question he asks is the day and hour of the seizure. If the patient was taken ill on a Saturday, the cause was distress of mind, heat of the blood, or the effect of an evil eye. Whatever the patient may say, he will be told that his symptoms will be headache, palpitation of the heart, thirst, restlessness, discomfort, and sleeplessness. The treatment prescribed by rule is the performance of the ceremony of almsgiving and of propitiatory rites, and the administration of a charm. This must be written on a plate and washed off and the liquid swallowed. The disease will last seven days, and if the treatment is properly carried out the patient will recover.

For each day of the week some special cause is assigned for the complaint; it is more often said to be supernatural than natural, and the treatment includes incantations, charms, and propitiatory rites, with the use of flowers, sugar, camphor, butter, coloured rice, the blood of fowls and goats, and the lighting of lamps. All these have a heathen origin and are unknown among the Muhammadans of other lands.

If death follows on this ignorant superstitious treatment of the sick, the Muslim consoles himself with his fatalistic creed. It is Kismet—the will of Allah. Fate is all-powerful; life and death are in the hands of God; good luck cannot be bought nor ill luck averted. A fable illustrating this is given by Ramaswami Raju in his *Indian Fables*.

A Rajah asked his Dewan if he believed in luck.

"I do," replied the Dewan.

"Can you prove it?" said the Rajah.

"I believe I can," was the reply.

The Dewan attached a parcel to a cord and hung it to the ceiling of a room in the palace. The parcel contained peas mixed with diamonds. He picked out two men. One of them believed in luck and never troubled to exert himself or to do any work that was not forced upon him. The other discredited luck and pinned his faith to human effort. They were asked to pass the night in the room, and on the following morning they would be rewarded for their compliance with the Rajah's wishes.

The man who believed in luck wrapped himself in his blanket and laid himself down to sleep. The other took a look round the room and discovered the packet. He was filled with curiosity as to its contents and never rested till he had pulled it down. There was not light enough to examine the contents very closely. As far as he could judge from the feel of them, he concluded that the substances contained in the bag were peas and stones. He ate the peas and threw the stones at his companion, calling him an idle fellow and saying, "Here are pebbles for your idleness."

The believer in luck took the blows with equanimity, gathering the stones into a little heap and knotting them in a corner of his turban, so that at least they might not be cast at him a second time.

In the morning the Rajah and the Dewan came to see how the two men had fared. The Rajah observed that the parcel had been taken down and opened.

"You may depart," he said, "and for your reward you may each keep what you have taken from the bag that was tied to the ceiling."

The one walked off with nothing more than the peas he had eaten; the other carried away the diamonds. The Dewan turned to the Rajah saying:

"Sire, you see that there is such a thing as luck, but it is as rare as peas mixed with diamonds."

Fakirs are more often seen in the north than in the south of India, except at Hyderabad. The Deccan, being still under Muslim rule, welcomes the Fakir, and he finds no lack of patrons and supporters.

A Muhammadan Fakir in India differs entirely from a Hindu Sadhu in dress and habit and in ideal. He does not think it necessary to employ contortions and self-inflicted wounds to attain his end. He is content to live in idleness, except for the constant repetition of the Quran, which cannot be called labour. He comes and goes as he wills, wandering up and down the roads, and accepting alms in the character of a mendicant as well as a scapegoat for the sins of the giver. He is a law unto himself, and, like the Sadhu, he believes himself to be above sin. He becomes stained with the dust of travel, and in the eyes of the European is not a desirable or attractive person.

The Sadhu's dupiti, or sheet, worn round the loins, or drawn shawl-fashion over his shoulders in cold weather, when new is dyed ochre. With long use and little washing it becomes so murky that the ochre is scarcely discernible. The Fakir's dress consists of a parti-coloured cloak, patched until very little of the original garment remains. He glories in his patches—the more the better, since they show how long he has been a holy person.

Fakirs, Derwishes (who are not to be found in India), and all other Muhammadan mystics are called Sufis. The term Sufi, says Canon Sell, is probably derived from the Arabic word *suf* (wool), of which material the garments worn by ascetics used to be made.

The founder of Sufism rebelled against the cut-and-dried monotheism of Islam, the stiff unyielding ritual, the fixed and rigid law laid down by Muhammad, and he preached a nearer road to union with the Deity. Ever since then Sufism has attempted to bridge the gulf that lay between the God of a pitiless fate—whose compassion could not go beyond the law—and the aspiring man who in his human weakness longed for communion with the Deity in this world as well as the next. The end of Sufism, like Yogaism, is absorption in God, the loss of a separate and personal existence. This is illustrated in a story told by the founder of the Maulavi Derwishes.

"One knocked at the door of the beloved and a voice from within said, 'Who is there?' Then he answered, 'It is I.' The voice replied, 'This house will not hold Me and Thee!' So the door remained shut. The lover retired to the wilderness and spent some time in solitude, fasting, and prayer. One year elapsed, when he again returned and knocked at the door. 'Who is there?' said the voice. The lover answered, 'It is Thou.' Then the door was opened."

It was in a scoffing spirit against Sufism and myticism that Omar Khayyám wrote his poem counselling men to take that which was attainable while it was within their reach:

> Awake, my Little ones, and fill the Cup
> Before Life's Liquor in its Cup be dry.

Why should they wait for the end, which might be personal annihilation?

> There was a Door to which I found no Key:
> There was a Veil past which I could not see:
> Some little Talk awhile of Me and Thee
> There seem'd—and then no more of Thee and Me.

In common with the Sanyâsi the Fakir smokes, an intoxicating mixture into which Indian hemp enters largely. When under its influence he is supposed to be inspired with the divine spirit and be possessed of miraculous powers. His actions, good or evil, like the Sanyâsi's, are held to be sinless, and his desires must be fulfilled no matter what their nature may be.

When a Fakir with a great reputation for sanctity dies, a mausoleum is raised over his grave. Lights are burned on the tomb and offerings are made to the Fakir in charge, in the hope that the dead man will intercede with God for the worshippers.

There is a tomb of this kind in the Mount road, Madras, where the Muhammadans of Triplicane burn little oil lamps made with a floating wick in a cup of oil, and offer incense on earthenware saucers. Sometimes the tomb is adorned with wreaths of oleander blossom and jasmine. The use of flowers and incense and lights is common to Hindus and Muhammadans alike. It creates a similarity in their rituals which does not exist. It is apt to lead to the belief that the object of the ceremonies is the same. This is not so. The Muhammadan performs his ritual in the hope of obtaining the intercession of a human being who has passed into union with the God of Abraham and Ishmael; whereas the Hindu has no other end in view but the propitiation of a malignant spirit in the hope of averting disaster.

MUHAMMADAN BELIEF IN HEAVEN AND HELL

I died as inanimate matter and arose as a plant.
I died as a plant and rose again as an animal.
I died as an animal and arose as a man.
Why then should I fear to become less by dying?
I shall die once again as a man
To rise an angel perfect from head to foot.
Again when I suffer dissolution as an angel,
I shall become what passes the conception of man!
Let me, then, become non-existent, for non-existence
Sings to me in loudest tones: "To Him we shall return."

Masnawi (translated by WHINFIELD).

CHAPTER VIII

MUHAMMADAN BELIEF IN HEAVEN AND HELL

THE Muhammadan belief in a future life is infinitely more comforting than that of the Hindus. The Hindu faith in the future is that his rebirth on earth will depend for its conditions entirely on his own actions in a former birth and on the ceremonies performed by his son and grandson on his behalf. He may be born of rich parents of the highest caste; in such circumstances he will lead a life of ease and luxury. On the other hand, his lot may be very different, and he may re-enter the world as a beast of burden, to be starved, over-worked, and beaten. Still worse, he may exist as a crawling reptile or loathsome insect.

Whatever his fate, of one thing the Hindu is convinced: he will have deserved all he gets; he will have brought it on himself and there will be no way of escape, either by repentance on his part, or through the tender mercy of a pitying

Deity. The utmost he can hope for, if he is fortunate enough to have a son and grandson, is a slight mitigation of the evil.

Brahma, who fixed these laws of retribution for all creation and for all ages before the world was made, is believed to possess a transcendental nature, too lofty, too impersonal to admit of emotion. Pity, mercy, love, beneficence are the attributes of a personality. Brahma is impersonal, therefore he can have no personal attributes whatever.

The eternal circle of rebirths is a deadening, hopeless creed against which the thoughtful and enlightened Hindu of the present day is already beginning to rebel. He demands something better than this inevitable law of retribution. He asks for progress, not retrogression. If he must retain his faith in transmigration at all, the transmigration must not be governed by the law of retribution.

The doctrine of transmigration has crept into Muhammadanism; but it is not orthodox. It was not taught by the Prophet. The mystics—the Sufis, who have already been mentioned—introduced it; and it is embodied by one of their own poets in the lines which head this chapter. The doctrine does not upset the orthodox teaching of

A MUHAMMADAN BOY

He wears an embroidered waistcoat over his white calico coat. Underneath is a shirt and pair of long pyjamas. He is the son of a clerk employed in Government House, Madras.

Islam concerning the Resurrection and the Last Day.

Muhammadans believe in the resurrection of the body and in the coming of Antichrist, and in the second coming of Jesus, the Apostle of God; but they deny the divinity of Jesus. According to the Quran other strange events will take place which are not included in the Christian creed. All creation then living will die at the blast of Israfel's trumpet, and the Heavens will melt away. God will reconstruct the earth and bring all men to life again. He will then judge mankind. The Faithful will go to the right and enter Paradise. The Unbelievers will go to the left and be cast into Hell. The countenances of the good will become shining white, while those who have done evil will turn black.

The Muslim Paradise is of a material rather than a spiritual character. Every means will be at hand to gratify the human senses. Hell, too, will be a place of physical torment, into which the never-dying serpent and everlasting fire provide torture for the wicked.

Between death and the resurrection there is an intermediate state, during which two fierce-looking angels with black complexions and terrible blue eyes visit every man in his grave to examine him with regard to his faith in God and the Prophet Muhammad. Those whose consciences are clear and whose faith has never weakened need have no fear of Munkir and Nakir, as the two dread inquisitors are called; but infidels and those who have been careless of ceremonial during life have cause to tremble. For them the intermediate state will be full of uneasiness and trouble in the consciousness of the fate that is in store for them.

Hell is divided by Islam into seven divisions, with torments of different degrees for the various sinners. Heaven is also supposed to be divided into degrees of bliss. To show God's mercy towards His creatures and how it exceeds His just wrath against sinners, these divisions number eight, one more than those of Hell.

The cemeteries of the Muhammadans in Madras have nothing to attract. They are dreary, untidy enclosures containing square masonry tombs uninscribed and without ornament. In time the mortar and sun-dried bricks are affected by the sea air, and the monuments fall into disrepair. The materials are used again; or they crumble to pieces and are lost in the rank herbage and long coarse grass, which adds to the desolate, neglected appearance of the burial-grounds. At no time is it safe or pleasant to wander among the tombs. The tropical sun heats the masonry, and it becomes the haunt of lizards, snakes, and scorpions, besides swarms of ants and other creeping things. The Muslims themselves are not drawn to their burial-grounds. They believe in ghosts and jinns, and in the haunting presence of the two black recording angels who await the newly dead, ready to begin their dread examination; so the Musalman gives the cemetery a wide berth, and never enters that open gateway unless he is obliged.

When a Muhammadan is near death he is called upon to make the customary confession of faith:

"I confess that God is one, without a partner; that truly Muhammad is His servant and His apostle."

After death the corpse is duly laid out. Incense is burned, and the shroud is censed an odd number of times. Ceremonial ablutions of the body follow with prayers; and when all is ready the corpse, wrapped in grave-cloths, is carried on a bier to the open space in front of the mosque. The mourners gather round, and the Imam attached to the mosque holds a service of supplication, repeating set prayers which are followed by the mourners, who assume the prescribed positions, facing Mecca, the hands and feet arranged according to ritual, the eyes fixed upon the spot to be touched afterwards in prostration. Except for the substitution of the Prophet's name instead of the name of Jesus, many of the prayers might be used at any Christian burial. The three following are beautiful in their simplicity and humility.

"O God! forgive our living and our dead, and those of us who are present; and those who are absent; our women and our full-grown persons, our men and our women. O God! those whom Thou dost keep alive amongst us, keep alive in Islam; and those whom Thou causest to die, let them die in the Faith."

"O God! give us good in this world and in the next, and save us by Thy mercy from the troubles of the grave and of Hell."

"O our Lord! suffer not our hearts to go astray after that Thou hast once guided us: and give us mercy from before Thee; for verily Thou art He Who giveth. O God! Thou art the dead man's Master; and Thou createdst him; and Thou didst nourish him; and didst guide him toward Islam; and Thou hast taken his life; and

Thou knowest well his inner and outer life. Provide intercessors for us. Forgive him, for Thou art the Forgiver, the most Merciful."

Instead of saying Amen the congregation cries "God is great!" after these prayers. Then follows a longer profession of faith made by the mourners altogether on behalf of the deceased, ending in a prayer for God's mercy and forgiveness for the dead man.

The chief mourner then dismisses the assembly of friends with the words, "All have permission to depart." Some avail themselves of it. Others follow to the cemetery and remain to assist in the actual interment.

When the grave is dug a cavity is left to enable the dead to sit up and answer the examining angels. The dead man is placed in the grave with the face turned towards Mecca, and the mourners arrange clods of earth round the head. Then follows the interesting ceremony of throwing earth into the grave by all the company. It is done three separate times. With the first handful the mourner, quoting from the Quran, says: "From it (the earth) We created you."

With the second he quotes again, saying: "And into it will We return you."

With the third he quotes again, saying: "And out of it will We bring you a second time."

While the grave is being filled in and formed into the long narrow mound that is familiar to Christian and Muhammadan alike, the mourners repeat a prayer for protection against Shytan, the devil, whom they believe is waiting to welcome lost souls to Hell. Water is sprinkled over the mound, and a branch of the pomegranate bush stuck into the freshly turned earth.

Before the mourners leave the grave they exhort the dead man in a set exhortation to remember his faith and the coming of the day of judgment: for his examination is very near. Even as they speak they seem to hear the faint rustle of the dark wings of Munkir and Nakir as they hover over the grave eager for the inquisition.

The mourners retire a short distance, and once more repeat prayers to God to have mercy on the dead. By this time the angels, they believe, have entered the grave, and the dreadful inquisition has begun upon which hangs his future happiness or misery.

At the conclusion of the service, and before the dispersion of the congregation, the salaam is said:

"The Peace and Mercy of God be with you."

The people return home, their minds occupied and disturbed by thoughts of their dear one whom they have just committed to the grave. The night is one of trouble and unrest for the dead and for the living; and consolation is found by the living in alms-giving and in prayers constantly repeated that God may be merciful, and that the confession of faith may satisfy the recording angels.

Fidelity to God and His Prophet is the cardinal virtue by which the Muslim confidently hopes to enter Heaven. A want of faith and neglect of the ceremonial prescribed by the Quran are the greatest sins he can commit. Such irregularities as the breaking of the Christian and Jewish commandments regarding a man's duty to his neighbour are passed over by Munkir and Nakir, whose enquiry embraces only the keeping of the faith and the manner of doing it.

It seems that even when the recording angels have been satisfied, the way to Heaven is not easy to traverse. The road lies over a bridge so narrow that it is like the sharp edge of a knife. The faithful need have no fear; for dreadful as it appears they will be able to pass safely over it. For the unworthy, that is, the unfaithful, its razor edge will be impassable; they will fall into the abyss below and sink into the torments of Hell.

Of the future of women very little is said. The Muhammadan believes that all creation, wise and foolish, devils and beasts, insects and birds will rise at the last day. Women cannot therefore be excluded. Moreover the Quran says: "To the Faithful, both men and women, God promiseth gardens and goodly mansions in the Garden of Eden."

The Muslim woman cannot say after this promise that she is left without a ray of hope in a future life.

A SLAVE GIRL IN A RICH MUHAM-MADAN FAMILY

The so-called slavery is a domestic service which lasts a lifetime. Usually the slaves are well treated.

HINDUISM AND CASTE

When they divided Purushu, how many portions did they make?
What do they call his mouth and arms? What do they call his thighs
and feet?
The Brahman was his mouth, of both his arms was the Rajanya made,
His thighs became the Vaisya, from his feet the Sudra was produced.

(*Rig Veda*, X. 90, 11, 12.)

CHAPTER IX

HINDUISM AND CASTE

THE Hindus outnumber the Muhammadans in the Madras Presidency by a very large percentage. It seems strange that the smaller community, even though it was the conquering race at one time, should have survived absorption in the larger, after so many generations have passed. The uncompromising pride of race of the Muslims has had much to do with their preservation, and the exclusive caste system of the Hindus has tended towards the same end.

Before the laws of Manu were formulated, caste, if it existed at all, was a vague, unobtrusive institution. No mention is made of it in the Vedas except in the foreshadowing said to be shown in the above lines. The legend runs that Purushu, the supreme deity, sacrificed himself and permitted himself to be cut into four parts. From those four parts sprang the four original castes, Brahmans, Kshatrias, Vaisyas, and Sudras.

There must always have been since the birth of man the distinctions that inevitably result from the varying conditions of life. The owner of flocks and herds was held to be in a superior condition to the man employed to tend those flocks and herds. A difference of position must equally have existed in the family and tribal circle, where one man was by primogeniture or by common consent acknowledged to be the head of the family or the tribe; but there is nothing to show in history that one community claimed superiority sufficient to refuse the admission of another community to a share in its religious rites and social ceremonies.

It was not until the Aryans had established themselves in the country that the caste system was evolved. In its inception it was racial in character. The ruling race separated itself from the conquered race. At the same time this separation was influenced unconsciously by trade; and the groups formed themselves into primitive trade guilds, protective of trade interests.

Thus it came about that when Manu tabulated his laws he found sufficient ground in existing custom to legislate on the subject. The descendants of the Aryan conquerors claimed caste distinction. The descendants of the conquered were denied the privilege of caste. They were deemed people of no caste. Among the Brahmans were men of letters learned in the legends of their mythology. They were quick to appropriate the parable of Purushu, and discover in the division of his body a divine origin of the institution of caste.

It was not for the conquered to refuse the ordinances of the conqueror. The Dravidians and the aborigines, whom the Dravidians had dominated, accepted the decree of the Aryans, and bowed to Manu's Laws without struggle or protest. The fetters were thus forged once and for all, and they still exist, although ages have passed. They remain a puzzle to the politician as well as to the missionary and the traveller.

It is said in the present day that with the introduction of Western thought and Western ways, caste is weakening. If caste were purely social—*which it is not*—this might be the case. The educated Hindu is not blind to the evils which have crept into the system. In the matter of exclusive feeding, exclusive marriage, the arbitrary and cruel laws of widowhood, and the sanctioned prostitution practised in the temples of the South in the name of religion and caste, he not only feels a national shame, but he would welcome reform. Some of the rules of caste have been affected by railway travelling and sea voyages; but not for a moment has the Hindu abandoned caste, or allowed it to relinquish its hold upon him. As the Rev. J. A. Sharrock says in his *Hinduism Ancient and Modern*, "The spirit of caste is just as strong as ever."

The reason for its tenacity of life is its nature. Caste *is* religion, in that it is the ritual of personal Hinduism.

The Hindus are notoriously a religious people, with a strong leaning towards superstition in their observances. Religious ritual enters into every domestic action, even down to the washing of the teeth and the consumption of food. The invocations and oblations made during the chief meal of the day by the head of the house, and the silence preserved by the family circle while eating, deprive the partaking of food of all sociability. It is nothing less than a religious ceremony, with the head of the family as priest.

In the same way the invocation and hymn of

praise to the deity which accompanies the performance of the toilet in the early morning of both men and women, makes the ablutions a religious ceremonial rather than a domestic office.

The simple act of lighting the lamp at night is done with an obeisance and the repetition of a sentence in which the deity is acknowledged as the fountain of light, the controller and lord of the sun. By repeating that sentence the mistress of the house not only conforms to a caste rule, but maintains her right to be regarded as head of the zenana as well.

The Brahmans have for ages past fed and nurtured this tendency on the part of the people to invest every act with religious significance. The consequence is that the Brahman's services are in constant requisition throughout a man's life. From the earliest period to the recurring anniversaries of his death the priest is required to sacrifice, the guru to teach and enquire into personal conduct, and the purohit to repeat prayers and present offerings taken to the temple. A large number of Brahmans are necessary to perform these offices—offices, be it remembered, that command fees. The most trifling ceremony has to be paid for. If the family is poor the fees may be small; but if rich they are demanded in proportion to the wealth of the householder.

Any action on the part of the political administrator of the country or of the missionary that is likely to undermine this need for the Brahman is resented by the twice-born; who, in self-defence, is working harder for the preservation of caste than he has ever worked before. As long as the Hindu religion lives, so long must caste endure, and the Brahmans will dominate the masses with their presumptuous claim to superiority.

Since the time of Manu the four great divisions have been undergoing a process of splitting up and subdividing until the divisions are too numerous to count. In this separation the people have been influenced by trade rather than by religion. Some trades being considered more honourable than others have taken precedence; and such is the force of example, the members of the more honourable callings hold themselves rigidly aloof from religious and social intercourse with the inferior, as the Brahman himself holds aloof from the castes of Sudra origin.

In Southern India the Kshattriya or soldier caste, the Rajanya of the Rig Veda, is not found; nor is the Vaisya, the merchant caste. Many of the merchants and shop-keepers of the south are of Sudra extraction. So also are some of the agriculturists. Others are pariahs, although they would like to be thought Sudras if they could only persuade people to believe it. Pride of birth is not confined to the nobility in India, nor to the Brahman. Many a pariah who has grown rich in trade and been able to afford to bring up his sons to some profession, or to put them in Government service, has disowned his pariah ancestry and claimed that his caste was distinctly not of out-caste origin.

There is still existing throughout the length and breadth of India a village system such as prevailed in England in the old feudal days. The over-lord of a district or parish retained among his dependents a carpenter, blacksmith, bricklayer, stonemason, shepherd, swineherd, and other workmen. They received a subsistence allowance in kind and were given house-room and other privileges, in return for which they rendered service to the over-lord and his establishment. The system vanished with the feudal lord, but left its traces in the entourage of the country squire. Large estates still employ their own work-people, the wheelwright, blacksmith, and carpenter, who are given quarters, usually in the form of cottages, and who are paid a weekly wage. The system is slowly dying out and will disappear altogether in England in time.

In India it is neither dissipated nor weakened by modern progress. It still exists completely organised, whether on a large or a small scale. The greater villages and up-country towns have their full complement of officials—magistrate, deputy-collector, etc.; professional men—vakil, schoolmaster, physician, priest, etc.; and tradesmen —goldsmith, carpenter, etc. These form the village. In hamlets there may be only two or three different artisans, the washerman, cultivator, and sweeper. Then the services of the stone-mason, well-digger, or carpenter must be sought in the nearest village.

Dr. Heyne, who was in the service of the East India Company, wrote a description of the Indian village community more than a hundred years ago. That description still holds good and is true in all its detail. He speaks of payments made regularly every month to the different members—the headman, accountant, barber, and others mentioned above. They each received a small sum in money or in kind from every household.

A HINDU PARIAH BEGGAR

He is too old to work or follow any trade.

In return they all gave their labour where it was required.

The workman is not dependent solely upon his monthly wage. There are an infinite variety of ways of obtaining perquisites. The wood provided by the agriculturist for the bullocks' yokes or for the primitive wooden ploughshare is in the rough. The trimmings and shavings are retained by the carpenter. Out of them he shapes wheel-spokes, linch-pins, legs for stools, ladles to stir the seething rice in the earthen pot; and these he sells to the villagers.

Madras city outside the limits of Fort St. George and Georgetown is made up of such villages. Large towns like Trichinopoly, Tanjore, and Madura are nothing but villages on a very large scale with colonies of tradesmen instead of a single family. Each colony has its assigned quarter, its separate temple and pujaris, its wells and its tanks.

T. B. Pandian in his book, *Indian Village Life*, gives no fewer than a dozen different professions and seventeen trades to a large village. They all conform to the traditional rule of the village system, never demanding socialistic changes either in condition or in circumstance. The sweeper, the lowest and most degraded of the outcastes, does not dream of placing himself on an equality with the carpenter; and the carpenter, although he assumes the Brahman thread, has no thought of equality between himself and the Brahman purohit attached to the village temple.

We of the Western world may bestow our pity on the outcaste shoemaker and sweeper, and spend our scorn on the presumptuous Brahman and goldsmith and carpenter. Neither the one nor the other is in the least affected by the stranger's pity or scorn; nor are they stirred to any sense of injustice. The sweeper enjoys life every whit as much as the Brahman. He laughs and revels in the village amusements with as much zest and appreciation as the goldsmith and carpenter; and he is born, married, and buried with as much ceremony and consideration from his fellow-outcaste men as the noblest of the twice-born.

Envy does not trouble him any more than it troubles the man in the streets of Madras who watches the Governor pass in state with his body-guard of lancers. He lives the time-honoured life of his forebears, bringing up sons and daughters to his lowly and undignified calling. If by chance he is asked whether his trade satisfies the ambition natural to all human beings, he shrugs his shoulders, lifts his hands (palms outward), and wags his head in assent to the momentous question, saying, "What is written on a man's forehead by the gods cannot be rubbed off."

OLD PARIAH WOMAN BEGGING

Her cotton sari is in rags and the coarse red blanket very dirty in spite of its picturesqueness.

THE HINDU VILLAGE SCHOOL AND TEMPLE

If I were asked, I should say that sacrifice, not pantheism, is the core of the Vedas; that transcendentalism, or a mystic philosophizing leading to agnosticism, is the substance of the Vedanta; that *karma* and transmigration, with the worship of Vishnu and Siva, tinged with the Vedanta philosophy, are the chief features of modern Hinduism of the higher castes; and that idolatry, sacrifices, animistic cults, devil-dancing, and so forth are the characteristics of the Hinduism of the lower castes and outcastes.

Hinduism Ancient and Modern (SHARROCK).

CHAPTER X

THE HINDU VILLAGE SCHOOL AND TEMPLE

EVERY large village has its poet. His claim to the title hangs on his command of words rather than on the power to express himself in poetical language. In the days when men could neither read nor write, it was the duty of the so-called poet of the village to relate the mythological and historical traditions handed down to him by a long line of ancestors. The object was to amuse and beguile the time when the work of the day was over, as well as to keep alive in the memory of the present generation the heroic deeds of gods and men in the past.

In these modern times the services of a reciter of epics are not really required for the purpose. Learned men of the West have translated the old books of the East from the little-known classical Sanscrit into English. From English it has been an easy task to turn them into the vernaculars.

Every one who can read in his mother-tongue may enjoy the Homeric Mahabharata and Ramayana; study the primitive religion of the Vedas; repeat the divine hymn of praise to be found in the Bhagavad-Gita; contemplate the complex philosophies of the Upanishads, and dip into the alluring mysticism of the Tantras.

Although the Hindu poet is no longer of any importance in the town, he is still welcomed and supported in the up-country village, where books are rare and libraries find no place. His art is not confined to the recitation of poetical traditions and tales, for which he receives his dole from the villagers. He, like the tailor, washerman, and carpenter, seeks to add to his income. There can be no perquisites in his profession. He falls back on his art, and makes a profit by working on the feelings of human nature. He composes elegies in praise of his richer neighbours; and in return he looks for small gifts in money or in kind—donations that can well be spared from the plenty of a prosperous household. A little rice, a few vegetables and fruits, a cast-off cloth or turban are received with gratification, and the poet is amply rewarded for his doggerel verse, in which he has unblushingly compared his patron's wife to an elephant—the highest form of praise to be given to a Hindu lady—and his sons and daughters to the moon and stars. No words are too extravagant when he is sure of his reward.

If, on the other hand, the rich man is mean and refuses to bestow largesse, the poem assumes another complexion and is full of virulent abuse. Such abuse could only be fulminated by one who was in total ignorance of the law of libel. The poem is not put into print, but it is read aloud in the village under the big banyan or tamarind tree, where the villagers congregate after work. The poet is probably not the only one to resent the meanness of the "squire." Others have experienced it, and the invective is received with shouts of laughter and a chorus of assenting "Ahahs!" Rather than be held up to public contempt and scorn, the big man prefers to pay for silence.

The poet sometimes acts as schoolmaster in remote villages where a Government aided, and consequently an officially supervised, school is not provided.

The pial school, as the unaided village school is called, is a very ancient institution. The curriculum includes nothing but the three R's in the simplest and most primary form. Instruction is given in the village rest-house, the chuttrum; or in a house that has been built by the villagers themselves for the purpose. No furniture is required. The pupils sit on the floor and learn to write with the forefinger in fine sand sprinkled round them.

When they become adept they provide themselves with pieces of dried palm-leaf and inscribe the leaf by means of a little sharp-pointed stylus inserted under the thumb nail. The few books used in the village school are made of rectangular pieces of palm-leaf inscribed in this manner and bound together with string between two bits of board the size of the palm-leaf. When not in use the books hang on nails in the wall, a safer means of preserving them from white ants than storing them on book-shelves.

As soon as the sun rises the pupils run off to school, returning home for their meals. The Hindu boy shows very little desire to play truant. Even if he does not like his lessons he comes to them willingly all the same, in consequence of his anxiety to learn.

The boys spend about nine hours of the day at the schoolhouse. The master gives them his attention only half that time. He leaves the elder pupils to teach the younger by a process of constant repetition that imparts a parrot-like knowledge requiring little or no effort of the brain. The monitors, in teaching from the book, teach themselves.

The advantage of the system of pupil teachers was recognised by Dr. Bell, the Superintendent of the Civil and Military Schools in Madras at the end of the eighteenth century; and he introduced it there. When he returned to England he advocated its use in English schools, and it was adopted throughout the kingdom.

The system works admirably where there is supervision. In the pial schools the pupil teacher has no supervision, and abuse creeps in. He is often unjust and cruel, favouring some boys and bullying others. The schoolmaster himself is not above reproach in this matter. An extra payment of a few pence from the rich man will command a larger share of instruction than the son of the poor man can obtain. It will also secure immunity from punishment which, if the truth be told, is more or less of the nature of torture than proper correction. In this respect, however, the schoolmaster is no different from the parents of the children, who have a variety of ways of inflicting pain and discomfort. Such barbarity would assuredly bring them within reach of the law if practised in Great Britain.

A great deal has been done by the British Government to improve the pial school and make it more efficient, by inspection and the giving of grants-in-aid where certain prescribed conditions can be fulfilled. The course of instruction remains elementary; but the teacher has qualifications which the self-taught poet-schoolmaster never attained.

The missionary societies have also assisted in the good cause of education and have supplied qualified teachers in well-equipped schools of their own; but there still remain many pial schools in remote villages where abuses linger and the children suffer from incompetent and bad-tempered teachers.

Every village has its temple dedicated to one of the many gods or goddesses of the Hindu pantheon. If the hamlet is too small to support a building worthy of the name of temple, it will have its devil-stone set up under the largest tree. The setting up of such a stone has frequently led in the past to the founding and building of many a temple that now has its imposing courts, its massive walls, and its solid towers.

It is brought about thus. A piece of ill-luck happens to an artisan or an agriculturist—a tool breaks; or a cart-wheel comes off; or a valuable cow dies. The magician is consulted—for a fee—and he declares that it is the work of a demon. Propitiatory pujah must be done or more mischief will be perpetrated. He assigns a tree to the devil as its residence, directs the frightened villagers to build a platform under it and set up a stone—a boulder about the size of a football is usually chosen—which he proceeds to worship.

The people contribute offerings and the stone is anointed with oiled butter. The pujari garlands it with flowers and prostrates himself before it in the belief that the spirit has taken up its residence in the shapeless block of gneiss.

Thenceforward the people take care that the puja shall be continued periodically; and there is never wanting a pujari to receive fees and offerings on behalf of the devil.

The spot is next enclosed, and a canopy is erected over the stone. Then the stonemason of the village is directed to fashion out a rude image in his spare moments. When it is finished it is set up with a beating of tomtoms and much feasting; and it is hoped that the demon will be so well pleased with his new residence and the worship offered him that he will refrain from injuring the villagers and their property.

A canopy is erected over the figure. First it is of bamboo and palm-leaf, but white ants and monsoon rains soon destroy it; and having had a good harvest through the kindness of their deity, who has refrained from being malignant, the people decide to erect a permanent building of sun-dried bricks or rough-hewn stone. A wedge-shaped tower rises above the roof, and thus the village temple comes into being. The offerings increase, and the visiting pujari finds it worth his while to make for himself a permanent residence behind the shrine. It was thus that the largest temple in South India had its origin, the Temple of Srirungam near Trichinopoly. The first enclosure with its low small building remains, the centre of a group of halls and courts, tanks and yards that cover more than seven acres.

Every demon thus honoured is said to be evil, whether male or female. Its attributes are of a human character, susceptible to human influences. The demon requires to be constantly propitiated by sacrifice, and to be kept in good-humour by offerings. It loves the smell and taste of blood, and enjoys—through the appetites of its attendants—the food provided by the worshippers.

Although the uneducated low-caste Hindu of South India worships evil spirits, he does not deny the existence of a deity who has a good and benevolent side to his nature. But the great All-Father is remote and impersonal, an abstract mystery requiring neither worship nor propitiation.

"Why should I worship the great All-Father?" asks the animist. "He will do me no harm. He needs no service, no sacrifice, no propitiation, I have nothing to fear from Him. It is the evil I have to consider; the devil who can do me harm and thwart me at every turn by sending fire or drought, flood or sickness upon me and my family."

Tell him that the devils are not gods; that the great All-Father is goodness and love without evil; he will reply—if he knows anything of his faith—that God is illimitable, and that therefore He must of necessity be good and evil. The power of evil, he believes, is coexistent and co-equal with the power of good.

In the south of India, Ganesa, the elephant god, and Hanuman, the monkey god, are frequently the titular deities of the temples. These are represented by the familiar half-human half-animal figures so often seen executed in brass. Kali, the dreaded goddess of cholera and small-pox, is another deity to whom numerous temples are dedicated. She is the wife of Siva, the destroyer; she has many names but only one nature, which is malignant and destructive.

The larger temples in the south are dedicated to Vishnu, Siva, and Krishna under the names of their different avartars. In every one is to be found the representation of the god. The image is made of a mixture of five metals, and it is enshrined in an inner sanctuary open only to the Brahman.

It is treated like a human being; washed and dressed and fed and duly marked with the sectarian sign used by its followers. Periodically it is adorned with embroidered garments and jewels; and it is brought out to be paraded with music and the beating of drums in the streets of the town. It must be understood that the image itself, a mere figure in inanimate material, has no virtue until the divine afflatus falls upon it; this, the Hindu believes, will only come through certain ceremonials. When once the rites have been performed, and the afflatus is supposed to rest

THE CAR FESTIVAL AT THE HINDU TEMPLE OF MYLIAPORE

The car is drawn along the road by enthusiastic worshippers who thus acquire merit and escape the consequences of their wrong-doing.

upon the image, the greatest care must be observed to avoid desecration. Many a riot and collision with the Muhammadans has occurred in the streets when the idol was being carried in procession.

Attached to the large temples are numbers of men and women who are supported by the endowment revenue and offerings. The men serve in various capacities connected with the ritual and also with the upkeep of the temple. The women are deva-dasis, servants of the god. They take part in the dances performed daily before the image, and sing hymns of praise during the ceremonial toilet. In the south they are all bound professionally to lead what is regarded from a Western point of view as an immoral life.

To them it is the performance of a religious duty, and in submitting to it they show themselves to be obedient servants of the deity. This strange subversion of one of our greatest moral laws is difficult for a European to comprehend. There is nothing immodest in the appearance or the behaviour of a dancing girl, as far as one can see. Europeans generally regard her dancing as a very poor performance. But when they come to understand the meaning of the movements and of the amorous words of her songs, they estimate her at her proper value as a daughter of shame and leave her severely alone.

Now, mark the topsy-turvydom of Hinduism. The Hindu honours the temple girl as a daughter of the deity; so great an honour is it regarded that the goldsmiths and weavers of Trichinopoly devote the eldest daughter of the family to the temple service of Srirungam. The girls are handed over young and are taught in the temple to read and write, sing and dance and dress themselves daintily, to adorn their hair with flowers and wear their jewels with dignity.

When they reach the age of thirteen they go through the ceremony of marriage with the god Subramanian, who is represented by a stone or image, or by a figure. After the ceremony they are ready to ply their trade with the devout worshippers who attend the temple. Their earnings go to swell the temple revenue.

A village temple has no women attached to it. At best it can only support its one resident pujari. He may or may not be of the Brahman caste. If a Brahman, he is frequently a pluralist and has charge of several temples, passing from one to another as his services are required.

If he is a non-Brahman, he conducts pujah for

the devil-stones in the neighbourhood, and practices as the Valluvan or village-seer and astrologer. His duties are not heavy, and he is not bound to any rigid ritual nor to any superior. He collects offerings, performs ceremonies connected with domestic events, casts horoscopes, fixes propitious days for beginning harvest or sowing the seed. He names the day when a journey may be safely undertaken; and he prescribes for the sick in much the same superstitious and ignorant manner as the Muhammadan seer.

He is ready to receive alms, manufacture charms, amulets, and love-philtres. He casts out devils, interprets dreams and omens. In all his transactions human cunning is employed, and the ignorance and childish imagination of his clients is worked upon. There is not a subject under the sun that he hesitates to pronounce upon.

Modern thought has given rise to scepticism, and the following story is frequently related in the villages:

A certain Rajah consulted an astrologer as to the length of his life.

"How long shall I live?" he asked of the wise man.

"Only two years; not more," replied the astrologer after consulting the Rajah's horoscope.

The prince was troubled; and the Dewan, seeing his distress of mind, said to the astrologer:

"How long will you live?"

"Twenty years or more," was the confident reply.

The Dewan drew his sword and cut off the head of the seer. Then turning to the Rajah he said:

"How is it possible for a man who does not know the time of his own death, though it was so near, to predict the time of your Highness's death? Take courage, and do not believe in superstitious men."

Although this story is so well known, the power of superstition is so great with the low-caste and out-caste Hindu, that the Valluvan flourishes and will continue to flourish for many years to come, not only throughout South India, but also in Ceylon; his impudent pronouncements will be received with credulity, and he will be liberally rewarded.

A HINDU DASI OR NAUTCH GIRL

She is attached to a temple and her earnings go to swell its revenues. The ornaments on neck, head, and arms are of gold. Those on the ankles and toes are of silver. However rich a woman may be her anklets and toe-rings are never made of gold. She dances on her heels with angular poses of the arms and hands.

DEVIL-DANCING

A devil-dance is like a garden of castor-oil plants. If once a man gets into it, it is difficult to get him out.

Hindu Proverb.

CHAPTER XI

DEVIL-DANCING

A DEVIL-DANCER is an animist. He inherits his religion with his dark complexion from a remote ancestry, pre-Aryan and of doubtful origin. He believes in spirits inhabiting trees, stones, etc. These mysterious powers are supposed to control certain spheres of influence that affect the fortunes of men. Being evil spirits and malignant in their disposition, they naturally delight in afflicting human beings with misfortunes. Therefore they have to be propitiated. The animist does not deny the existence of Brahma, the impersonal and unknowable god; but, as has already been said, he sees no necessity to worship so remote and unapproachable a deity.

The materialisation of spirits is a very ancient belief. It lingers in every religion, not excepting Christianity. The general idea running through it in all ages is that without the aid of a material body the spirit is unable to assume a personality through which it may experience the pleasure of emotion.

When Jesus Christ met the man possessed by the devil that bore the name of Legion, the evil one entreated Him not to disembody it; but to permit it to pass into the herd of swine—not one single individual of the herd, but into the whole company of pigs; which apparently was not too numerous to contain it; and the request was granted. We are told of the disastrous result, which could not have been anticipated by the devil, but was foreseen by our Lord when He acquiesced.

It has been suggested that certain signs and cabalistic figures were used in remote prehistoric days for the purpose of providing the evil spirit with a form for materialisation when it was evoked. By the power of these magical figures the demon was restrained from entering the human body and held in some subjection. In all ages a belief has existed in the varying strength of different evil spirits, some being small and weak and easily subdued, others possessing enormous power and requiring a whole family or species for embodiment. The modern spiritists of the West recognise this difference and call the lesser spirits elementals.

These elementals are known to the devil-worshippers of Southern India as "Ammas." They are female, as the name implies, and of a petty malignant disposition, more mischievous than malicious. They have a name prefixed to the "amma," which latter word means woman; "Chin-amma," little woman. They are provided with a stone or a block of wood or a brass pot of water for materialisation, and they are supposed to be easily mollified.

The greater devils—sometimes male and sometimes female—are more to be feared, being of greater strength and deeper malignity. They are not content to plague a single individual or household, but will scourge a village or whole district with disease or famine, fire, flood, or drought. In former days they were propitiated with human sacrifice. To-day their worshippers have to be contented with buffaloes and goats.

Through the agency of a stone or image they are believed to be able, like Krishna, Siva, and Vishnu, to enjoy the gratification of a gross human appetite.

Sometimes the evil spirit, tired of its tree and

stone, seizes upon the rash human being who approaches too near its haunt after sunset. It enters by the open mouth and possesses the man. The magician is summoned to drive out the "invader." His procedure is very like that already described as in use among the Muhammadans. The unfortunate subject is beaten. Incantations and fierce exorcisms are pronounced and charms manufactured. So strong is the power of hypnotism and suggestion on the impressionable and superstitious Oriental that a cure is often effected. The symptoms disappear and the patient recovers.

There is another kind of possession in which the man deliberately places himself at the disposal of the devil and becomes its willing medium, lending his body for indulgence in appetites that are unnatural and often horrible.

Such a man is here depicted.

By certain ceremonies he has rendered himself acceptable to his supernatural visitant; and by his own mouth he announces the arrival and installation of his terrible guest. Just such a man as this appears once a year in an important blood festival that takes place at Trichinopoly. He lends his body to the malignant female demon of a certain temple in the neighbourhood of the town. The building stands on the raised banks of a tributary stream of the Cauvery River. The image is brought out and carried in procession to a street in one of the suburbs of Trichinopoly, and it is placed on a platform erected in the street. The pujari, a cultivator of the Vellala caste of Sudra origin, comes forward, no one knows whence, and declares that the spirit has taken possession of his body. He places himself before the idol in a prominent position where he can be seen by the crowd that has gathered round. He is garlanded with strings of flowers something in the manner of the sketch. On his head he wears a fantastic head-dress; and his face is rubbed with sacred ashes and coloured powder. For the time he is as mad as he looks.

He stands upon a raised platform or is lifted to the shoulders of a couple of men so that he may be seen by the crowd while the sacrifice of blood is made. It is a disgusting ceremony from beginning to end. Hundreds of black goats are driven in from the villages. The animals are led up to the pujari singly. Water is sprinkled on the head, and as the creature shakes itself to throw off the drops, an attendant swings round a heavy sword and decapitates it with one blow. The bleeding head is caught up and presented to the pujari, who places his lips to the wound and appears to drink the blood.

The body of the goat is returned to the head of the family and a curry is prepared which is eaten as a love-feast by the party that has accompanied him. All night long the excited worshippers remain in the streets uttering staccato cries of "Ah! Hah!" drawing in the breath with the first syllable and sighing out the second.

The ceremony is continued throughout the day, the pujari receiving the heads eagerly as though the appetite of the demon were insatiable. His wild blood-shot eyes and his insensibility to the presence of the crowd point to the fanaticism produced by bhang and datura poison.

Devil-dancing is practised to a greater extent in the far south throughout the broad sun-bathed plains of the Peninsula where the palmyra tree abounds than in the north. The land stretches away on all sides in a dead level, and mirage paints on the horizon wide pools and lagoons where no water can be found. Whirlwinds dance over the plains, raising columns of golden dust laden with dead leaves and small stones. These whirlwinds are said to be the chariots of the devils, and the natives believe that the evil ones enjoy through the agency of the dust-storm the sensation of motion.

Every Friday night the people of Tinnevelly indulge in a devil-dance. The dancing is not restricted to ascetics or men connected with temple worship. The devil may "possess" any agriculturist or toddy-drawer of the Shanar caste.

Demons are believed to take up their residence in palmyra trees, the leaves of which have never been cut for toddy-drawing. Probably certain palms are left untouched so that the devils may not be wandering at large without a habitation. These evil spirits are supposed to be the ghosts of human beings, not elementals; in this respect they differ from the spirits worshipped in village temples and under the trees in North Tinnevelly.

The Shanars are very jealous of allowing their dances to be seen by strangers, the reason being that the afflatus will not rest on the dancer except in the presence of true believers.

Some years ago the curiosity of two English boys, the sons of an old missionary, was roused by what they had heard, and they determined to see one of these orgies. They hid themselves in an ancient banyan tree, under which a dance was to take place after sunset, starting early in the afternoon before the people had left off work. The trunk was hollow, and into this they crept, climbing to a cleft from which they had a good view without being seen. It was a dangerous exploit, for if they had been discovered when the company had already indulged in the quantity of arrack usually consumed, the consequences might have been fatal to the boys.

After the sun had set the people began to assemble. A fire was lighted and some torches prepared by tying rags to the end of sticks and soaking them in oil.

The musicians arrived with pipes and tomtoms,—the pipes producing a barbaric squealing. The devil-dancers, three in number, appeared dressed as in the sketch. Innumerable strings of beads and coloured shreds of cotton formed a kind of petticoat and mantle. On their heads they wore tall head-dresses made of the same material; and their faces were smeared with grey ashes. A glance at the picture will show the curious bent brows and heavy features, indicating a latent madness easily roused by any exciting cause. These men took up a position where the flickering light of the fire fell upon them.

The company formed a wide circle round the fantastic figures; the noisy chatter subsided as fear and awe of the supernatural fell upon everybody, young and old alike, and they waited for developments with breathless expectation.

The musicians began to play their panpipes and the drummers to beat their tomtoms. There is a peculiar manner of beating the tomtom in these assemblies which excites the dancer. It is said to be acceptable to the demon, who responds more quickly to its sound than to any other.

On this occasion the afflatus was slow in manifesting itself. The dancers moved on their heels, swaying now and then in rhythm with the beat of the drum, their streamer petticoats swinging with the motion as though blown by some mysterious wind. The people were strangely quiet and observant, like animals, watching partly in fear and partly with a fascinated curiosity.

This continued for some time, and the boys were beginning to think that devil-dances were somewhat overrated, when suddenly, without any warning, one of the dancers broke out of the measured step and began to move spasmodically.

This was a signal for the musicians to quicken the pace. The excitement increased and spread to the other performers. The evil spirits were awakening in them also. They swayed their bodies backwards and forwards, their loose hair and streamers sweeping to and fro and hiding their features from view. They spun round with an occasional wild quick leap, and the music raced more madly with their increasing activity.

The people recognised the presence of the demons by raising their voices in a shout of welcome. It was in the form of a prolonged cry, to which a tremulous character was given by a rapid touching of the lips or tongue with the palm of the hand. It is a noise that young children sometimes find pleasure in making. The reason for placing the hand before the mouth is to prevent the entrance of evil spirits into the body.

The shouting, drumming, squealing of panpipes, together with long melancholy blasts from tin horns, made the night hideous with sound and appalled the young listeners in the tree. The scene was nothing less than devilish, and the idle curiosity of the English boys was turned to horror, not unmixed with fear, at finding themselves in the middle of a large concourse of madmen. There was no escape. They would have to see the orgy through to the bitter end, and above all they

A DEVIL-DANCER OF SOUTH INDIA OF THE TODDY-DRAWER CASTE

His face is rubbed with ashes. His dress is composed of streamers of cotton, tassels of different colours, strings of beads, and tinsel. He is ready for the manifestation of the demon in his person. The afflatus does not fall upon him until after sunset. The ornament on the top of his headdress is the five-headed cobra.

must not lose their presence of mind. Needless to say, they had ample time to repent of their temerity.

During the dance arrack was freely drunk by the audience as well as the performers. The frenzy increased and the dancers turned and swayed and leaped like maniacs. Some of the company caught the infection. Men and women joined in the dance, bounding into the circle as insane for the time being as the professional dancers themselves. They tore their hair, clutched wildly at their garments, rending them and throwing them aside until they were left stark naked.

It was not until the small hours of the morning that the noise died down. The dancers fell exhausted and became unconscious. The company, overcome by drink and excitement, sank to the ground and fell asleep. The musicians followed their example. The torches went out and the fire died down. Darkness enfolded the scene and silence reigned.

The boys, trembling in every limb, crept from their hiding-place more dead than alive and sped home, carrying with them a memory that remained to the end of their days.

The devil-dancer is not confined to the palmyra

district. He makes a profession of his calling and passes on from village to village, organising a dance here and a dance there for the benefit of a big village or group of hamlets. It was one of these itinerant dancers who was thus caught in his war-paint and sketched.

The peon whose special duty it was to attend personally on Lady Lawley was the son of a devil-dancer. He has, however, abandoned the faith of his ancestors and no longer believes in devils that live in trees and stones and village temples.

The dance organised by the professional devil-dancer for the benefit of a district is preceded by a blood sacrifice at one of the village temples. The usual offerings are made of fruit, flowers, sugar, camphor, butter, and arrack. The dancer comes with his high headdress, brass ornaments, and bells, his person hung with streamers of coloured cotton, tinsel, and beads, to which are added sometimes ropes of oleander, jasmine, and marigold blossom. The blood of the fowl or kid is mixed with rice and the dancer professes to feed the devil with the abominable mixture, feigning to see the devil near him.

On his proclaiming the presence of the demon,

the worshippers fall to the ground in abject terror, shutting their eyes and mouths lest they should actually see the evil spirit and lest it should enter their bodies.

The dancer then runs to the burial-ground, a favourite haunt of demons in the East, followed by two attendants. He throws balls of his stained rice round him as he passes along the way, and presently returns to the people; they rise and receive some of the rice and also a handful of sacred ashes with which they smear themselves. Then follows a drinking orgy, with the drumming of tomtoms and squealing of pipes and blowing of horns. The dance which accompanies the music is similar to that seen by the two boys hidden in the old banyan tree.

On the following day another sacrifice of blood is made, and the people disperse to their homes with the comfortable assurance that they have acquired sufficient merit by their religious exercises to save them from the frown of the gods until the next devil-dance is organised.

In Ceylon the professional devil-dancer ranges up and down the island among the estate coolies, preying upon them and demanding fees from every family. There he adds a mask to his make-up, a hideous representation of the human face with gross exaggerated features painted in gaudy reds and yellows. The mask is supposed to be a likeness of the demon. For sheer repulsive ugliness it exceeds all European conceptions of the evil one, horns, hoof, and tail notwithstanding.

THOMAS, LADY LAWLEY'S PERSONAL PEON OR ATTENDANT

He is wearing his hill uniform of red cloth. He has exchanged his ancestors' superstitious faith for Christianity.

THE HINDU HOMESTEAD

A mud hut facing south is preferable to a terraced house facing north.

Hindu Proverb.

A VILLAGE SCENE IN KALBUNDIPORE, MYSORE, INHABITED BY CANARESE

It is typical of the hamlet or small village throughout the south of India. The houses are built of mud and thatched with dried palm leaf.

CHAPTER XII

THE HINDU HOMESTEAD

In every large village there are five castes following respectively five trades. The castes are linked although they do not intermarry, and they all claim descent from the Brahmans. On the strength of this claim they assume the sacred thread. They are not recognised by the Brahmans, however, nor are they allowed to intermarry with the twice-born nor join in their caste ceremonies. The legend of their origin is as follows:

In the old days there was a large town in the south of India which was the capital of a powerful kingdom. The village system ruled in the town, the different trades and castes being separated into communities by mutual consent. The goldsmith, carpenter, blacksmith, mason, and brazier or worker in brass congregated in a certain part of the city and built themselves houses. To ensure greater seclusion they erected a wall round their quarters. They prospered and grew rich, and with wealth came arrogance and independence.

The Maharajah of the country watched their increasing strength with uneasiness. He feared lest they should rebel against his authority, and he sent his troops to bring them into subjection. Accordingly an army appeared before the walls and demanded their submission. It was refused. The soldiers attacked the fortifications, but their operations were rendered useless by virtue of the magnetic quality of the stones that formed the bastions. The magical quality drew the swords and spears from the hands of all who approached.

A fort that cannot be subdued by assault may be conquered by guile. The commandant of the besieging force accordingly set himself to discover the secret. It was divulged through the wiles of a Delilah, a beautiful dancer, who with her troop of girls captivated the heads of the castes. They told her that the magic power of the loadstone could only be broken by fire. Fires were thereupon built under the walls which crumbled to pieces, and the fort was taken. The five castes were ruthlessly exterminated, root and branch.

In the course of a few years the inhabitants of the town discovered that their agricultural

A TAMIL GIRL

She is dressed for a visit with flowers in her hair and a handsome silk sari. She is not purdanashin.

implements, tools, cooking utensils, weapons, as well as their brass vessels, were wearing out and required renewing. They looked round for means of procuring new ones, but could find no one skilful enough to make them. In vain the townspeople who followed other trades endeavoured to imitate the skill of the five linked craftsmen. The basket-maker made baskets, the shoe-maker shoes, the well-digger dug wells, the oil-presser crushed out the oil, the farmer grew corn, and the cowherd supplied the town with milk and butter; but not one of them could shape the bullock yoke or fashion the cart-wheel or form the wooden plough-share. None could temper the raw metal and forge a pick-axe, a saw, file, or knife. Nor could any one be found to dress a block of stone with that cunning which permits the builder to dispense with mortar in building, nor to mould a brass tray or lota, nor to turn and engrave a fine gold bangle for a bride.

Then arose an outcry at the mistake made in the past in the annihilation of these five indispensable trades. The Maharajah was full of regret for his hasty action and did what he could to make amends. He offered a large reward for the discovery of a survivor of the extinct castes, who might by some fortunate chance have escaped the terrible fate of his fellows. Not a single individual could be found; they were all dead.

The Rajah sent a crier round the town with a branch of scarlet coral, offering a reward to any one who was able to thread it. Many tried their best, for the sum of money was large, but without success. The tiny tunnel that ran through the coral was too fine and tortuous for the clumsy fingers of the agriculturist, the basket-maker, herdsman, and followers of the coarser trades.

Living in the town was a Brahman shopkeeper who had married a woman from the loadstone fort. At the time of its destruction her sister happened to be visiting at the merchant's house. This sister gave birth to a child a few weeks later who was brought up as the chetty's son. The boy inherited the skill of his ancestors, and early showed himself to be clever with his fingers.

His mother brought the coral to him and giving him a piece of fine silk told him to thread it; but the task proved too difficult even for the fingers of a goldsmith's child.

The boy, defeated for the moment, remained seated in deep thought, idly watching the tiny red ants as they toiled in and out of the masonry of the verandah. Then he went to the storeroom and dipped the end of the silk in honey.

He placed the coral in the track of the ants and fixed it in the entrance of their nest. He had not long to wait. An ant took up the sweetened end of the silk and, after a vain endeavour to pass in otherwise, it entered the tunnel of the coral and drew the thread with it. Before the silk completely disappeared the boy lifted the coral and shook off the struggling ant. The task was accomplished and the coral threaded.

His mother claimed the reward. Her story was told to the Maharajah, and he presented her with a house and some land. She was ordered to supply her son with materials and give him every facility for following in the steps of his ancestors. The boy grew up and married his cousin, the daughter of his mother's sister by the Brahman. It was through her that his children subsequently claimed to be descended from the twice-born. There were five sons of the cousins' marriage. They followed the five lost trades respectively, and were called the Panchalar, from the Sanskrit word "panch," five.

The most degraded of the village callings is

that of the sweeper. It is strange to see in these progressive days the uncomplaining patience with which these people accept their fate and perform their duties, bringing up their children to the same thing. This resignation to fate is not found throughout India. In the Punjab the Chuhras, a section of the outcaste population, bitterly resent the ostracism imposed on them by the Hindus and Sikhs for whom they work.

In the south Indian villages the sweeper is poorly paid and often overworked. He is also despised and brought under open contempt on account of his trade. It is his business to carry away all the sewage of the village and to deposit it at a distance from the houses. In addition to his scavenger duties, he has to go errands for Government officials whose business brings them to the village.

Not only his touch but his shadow is pollution to the higher castes. He must step aside off the road, putting a prescribed distance between himself and the approaching Brahman. It is his duty, not the Brahman's, to observe the rule, and any breach of it is visited on the unfortunate pariah's head by corporal punishment. On no account may he draw water from any well but his own. If he is

A PARIAH WOMAN WITH A BASKET CONTAINING THE MORNING'S MARKETING

She wears no ornaments—not because she is poor, but because she is a widow. The pariahs do not shave the heads of their widows.

thirsty in the heat of the day, he must beg from those who have the right to use the public well, and he must wait until pity moves some one to pour a little water into his cupped hands.

A movement is on foot to better the condition of the great mass of the outcaste people. They form a fifth of the population of India. Although they are all reckoned to be outside the pale of caste, they have divided and subdivided themselves through the long ages into what they term castes; and they observe the divisions rigidly. The pariah domestic servant is an outcaste in the south, but he holds himself to be infinitely superior to the sweeper and the worker in leather, with whom he will neither take his food, nor intermarry, nor join in the practice of religion. This caste distinction, whether among the highest or the lowest of India's millions, is one of the chief difficulties in the path of the missionary.

The woman in the sketch is a market coolie. She brings home the meat and vegetables purchased by the cook in the bazaar. The cook is also a pariah. No caste native would employ him or his market woman.

The touch that makes the whole Hindu world kin is in the observance of religious rites. Nothing is done or even projected without the assistance of the seer and the pujari—the one to interpret the will of the deity and point out the right course to pursue to avoid misfortune; the other to propitiate with sacrifice and offerings that the favour of the gods may be obtained.

The life of the Hindu, from six months before his birth to his death and three generations after, is honeycombed with religious ceremony. The building of his house, the cultivation of his land, the buying and selling of his merchandise, the working of the loom, the blessing of the implements and tools of every description, all these require sacrifice and offerings at the hands of the pujari.

Religious rites are enjoined for every domestic event, birth, death, and marriage, and they follow a man to his grave in the shraddah ceremonies performed by his descendants for three generations. The Hindu servants have been laughed at for the frequency with which they ask for a holiday "to bury my grandfather." It is not to bury but to keep the anniversary of the burial with certain rites that are propitiatory and which will benefit the dead man when he is reborn on this earth. The Brahmans understand the reason for these ceremonies. The lower classes imitate without

A HINDU WOMAN

She is wearing handsome coloured glass bangles, gold ear-rings, a gold necklace and another of coral beads. To the latter is attached her Thali or marriage badge, the equivalent to the wedding-ring.

knowing much of the doctrine underlying the action.

The appearance of an Indian house suggests the idea that it must have been built haphazard. It often stands crooked with the line of the street, and frequently its chief entrance is at the side or back instead of in the road.

The dwelling of a landowner or prosperous tradesman or money-lender is usually near the centre of the village. It is made of sun-dried bricks. Its roof may be tiled or terraced. Whatever direction the street in which it stands may follow the kitchen must face north. Indian houses have few windows; many have none at all. Light enters by the doors. The door of the kitchen opens into a walled or enclosed garden, where vegetables are grown. It is the most important, most jealously guarded room in the house. Here the food is prepared; and the *lares and penates* of the household are preserved in a small cupboard ready for the daily worship; they are brought out by the master of the house, who makes an oblation of food and drink before beginning his own meal.

A storeroom is attached or built close by, where grain is kept. The camphor-wood boxes containing the clothes and jewels of the family sometimes stand in the storeroom; but if there is easy access from outside, personal property is stored in the women's rooms and jewels are buried under the floor.

A second door in the kitchen leads into the courtyard, which is the centre of every house that is not a mud hut. The yard may be very small or it may be spacious. It is of great importance as being the only place where purdanasheen women can get a breath of fresh air.

At the end of the courtyard is a hall, which serves as a living room during the day and a sleeping chamber for the men at night. The front door is in the south wall of this hall. Visitors and friends of the same caste are allowed to enter, but all others are rigidly excluded. If the master of the house has occasion to receive a visit on business from a man of lower caste and not a pariah, he interviews him in the pial or raised verandah outside the front door. If the man is a pariah, he stands in the street at a fixed distance, which he may on no account pass, and the owner of the house carries on the conversation in shouts, or by means of one of his own servants as a messenger.

No outcaste is permitted to build a house of this description that requires beams. If he dared

A CORN MERCHANT

His wares consist of maize, two kinds of gram (beans), rice of different qualities and a fine grain called millet. The staple food of the Canarese is millet which is called ragi. The Tamils eat a small grained rice that boils a greyish white. Horses and cart-bullocks are fed on gram. The maize is roasted and chewed as a luxury.

to be presumptuous enough to put wooden beams instead of bamboo rafters into his roof, his house would straightway be pulled about his ears and he would be beaten, even though he might be able to buy up the whole village.

An Indian dwelling requires very little furniture; a cot, pillows, and rugs, mats, a few stools, and plenty of brass pots and dishes, suffice for the family of the greatest village magnate.

The life of the household is essentially a community life with little or no privacy; this tells against the domestic happiness of a son when he brings home his bride. He is given a small room opening into the courtyard—perhaps it is added when he marries—for his sleeping chamber and for storing his few personal effects; but he is not allowed by the voice of custom to use it as a sitting-room, nor by the same unwritten law is he permitted to converse with his young wife during the day. Her time is fully occupied from morning to night in the preparation of the food in the kitchen under the eye of her mother-in-law.

The villagers who have smaller means than the landowner or merchant build less pretentious houses. Some are nothing but mud huts with only one room, which is used as a kitchen, a corner is screened off for the women and as a storeroom. In the dry months the men spread their mats outside under the walls of the house. They roll themselves in a blanket or sheet, enveloping their heads as well as their bodies to protect themselves from the mosquitoes. Their pillow is a block of wood hollowed out in the upper part to make a head-rest. They lie down after dark and get up before dawn.

Every house or hut has an outer yard if it is possible. Houses in streets have verandahs attached instead of the yard. In the agricultural districts there is a lean-to shed for cattle. Where space is available a vegetable garden is made. Every hut, however small and lowly, has its gourd vine sprawling in picturesque, luxuriant growth over mud wall and thatched roof, displaying a glorious patch of emerald green in the golden sunlight.

In front of the door of house and hut the women, after sweeping the mud-plastered ground, draw geometrical patterns with no little skill in white chalk, and ornament the design with the yellow flowers of the gourd. Even this trifling act is not without its religious significance, an act to propitiate and please one of the many deities.

Rude pottery figures crudely coloured are to be seen on many of the roofs. They are put there to divert the evil eye from the house itself. The inverted earthenware pots, white-washed and spotted over with black, serve the same purpose in the fields while the crop is growing and ripening.

Every household is ruled by the head of the family. He owns most of the household effects and the clothes and jewels. He is bound by the same unwritten law of custom to extend his hospitality to any member of the family who through ill-health or misfortune may need help. By the practice of this admirable rule, each family supports its own poor. Begging in the streets is a profession which any one may join if he chooses, but it is not a resort for the destitute.

The mother or wife of the head of the house rules in the kitchen. By virtue of her position it is she who performs the daily religious ceremony connected with the lighting of the lamp at sundown. After it is lit she prostrates herself before it and rubs some sacred ashes on her forehead as she repeats a few words of praise to the deity. The rest of the women on seeing the lamp follow her example.

The members of an Indian household are busy

all day except during the midday hour of sleep after dinner. Rich and poor alike go through their domestic duties without haste, cooking, pounding, and cleaning rice, grinding curry-stuff, and looking after their babies with much talking and laughter, varying it with quarrelling and weeping, and sometimes with a tearing of each other's hair and the use of the stick. Their voices are often raised to a high pitch, and they exercise very little restraint when moved by emotion. The conversation is of a personal character, the language being more expressive and outspoken than refined or polite. They are without education; and while the boys run off to the village school, the girls are taught to take part in domestic duties as soon as they can run and talk.

There are two things in the East that are essential for feminine success. One is maternity; the other is capacity for cooking. Looks do not matter, nor figure nor dress. Woman's power lies in motherhood and in making or superintending the making of a good curry.

A tale that is often told under the big tree in the centre of the village, and which raises shrieks of laughter, is to the effect that once upon a time a man reproached his wife with having so little to do.

A BETEL-LEAF AND ARECA-NUT SELLER

Betel is the pan supari of the north. The leaf grows on a pepper-vine which is often planted for support with a young tree yielding a leaf used in curry. The acrid areca-nut is sliced and enclosed in the leaf with a pinch of powdered lime. It is stimulating and causes a flow of the saliva.

"Your work is nothing compared with mine in the fields. What is the boiling of rice and the making of a curry? It is of no consequence."

"Very well; we shall see about that!" replied the indignant wife.

The next day when he returned from a fatiguing morning in the fields, instead of a savoury curry, piles of boiled rice, and saucers of tempting green chutney, he found raw mutton, raw rice, unground curry ingredients, pepper, ginger, coriander seed and cocoa-nut, and a pot of butter. They were neatly arranged on green leaf platters.

"What is this?" he cried angrily. "Am I to have no dinner?"

"There is your dinner, husband," she replied, pointing to the unappetising array. "Since you declared that cooking was of no consequence, I thought it unnecessary to trouble about it."

The village system is little understood by the peoples of the West. It is an example of what home rule can do if confined strictly to the area of village government. Offences against the unwritten law of the community are tried by the punchayet, the village council. The five members of the council are chosen from among the chief men of the place. They give their services gratis, and they hold their sittings in the public rest-house after working hours. Disputes concerning land, division of property, temple affairs, quarrels, divorce, and differences between the various tradesmen and the customers who have the right to their services come before the punchayet.

The proceedings are as primitive and simple as they were a thousand years ago. The watchman calls up the plaintiff, who states his case. He is followed by the defendant and the witnesses for both sides.

The court is cleared after the hearing and the five members sit in conclave. As soon as a verdict is arrived at—a majority verdict suffices—judgment is pronounced. Then they call in the party who has lost his case and give him a scolding interlarded with plenty of abuse. He is fined in cocoa-nuts for the village temple deity, and in rupees which go to the village fund.

It is an admirable system too often neglected in these days of progress and rapid locomotion. Where the railroad helps them, the people are taking their cases to the magistrate's court. There they are preyed upon by the swarms of vakils (lawyers) who haunt the courts, and they are ruined. The punchayet costs nothing; it is

A BARBER

He is called by the Hindus "the son of the village," as he is as necessary an institution as the dhoby or washerman. No man in the East shaves himself except the Englishman. In the village the barber's methods are primitive and barbaric. His customers emerge from his hands sore and wounded. He also practises surgery; and his wife is a nurse and midwife. Their ways in these branches of medicine are on a par with the shaving operations.

prompt in its action and very equitable. Above all, it thoroughly understands the people it deals with, their language and method of thought, and it is not likely to err through a misunderstanding of the village conditions.

Each village is complete in itself with its caste system and customs; and in its completion it is invulnerable to the shafts of the socialist propagandist. But its isolation destroys to a great extent interdependence between itself and other villages. In spite of its marvellous internal cohesion, it cannot join with other villages in promoting a common cause. To form a big labour party or a strong trades' union, the various castes would have to be broken up and the village disintegrated. Caste would have to be abolished, and the despised sweeper and shoemaker admitted to the same privileges as those enjoyed by the blacksmith, carpenter, and mason.

Although the Hindu enjoys a very ancient system of home rule, the day of social equality is still very far distant from rural India.

VILLAGE AMUSEMENTS

There is a season for everything; for eating and sleeping; for working and playing. The bamboo must be cut when the moon is waxing or it will be good for nothing.

Hindu Proverb.

CHAPTER XIII

VILLAGE AMUSEMENTS

THE inhabitants of an Indian village work patiently and without haste from sunrise to sunset, asking for no eight-hour day or weekly half-holiday. The deliberation with which they undertake their tasks and their inert method of labouring is apt to irritate a stranger, accustomed to the strenuousness of the West. Hustle is unknown in the East. "Haste is of the devil; only bad men run," says the Oriental.

The hours of labour depend entirely on the sun. There is not the same variation in its rising and setting as in the West, and no necessity arises for using artificial light. After the midday meal, when the sun is at its zenith, all nature rests in the tropics. It is called "black man's holiday," a holiday that is not despised by the European himself, although he does not keep such long hours in his office as the villager keeps in his field or workshop.

This leisurely way of taking life leaves the villager healthily weary, but not overworn at the end of the day. After his evening meal, he saunters to the general gathering-place in the centre of the village, where the poet has probably seated himself already and begun a recitation in a nasal sing-song voice that penetrates to the outer circle of listeners.

If there is a moon, the villager watches the young men dancing or testing their strength in friendly wrestling. The women, sitting apart in groups, look on and gossip, until sleep sends them home to seek their mats and pillows. The moon in India shines with a brighter light than in the temperate zone; and, except when the monsoons burst, it is seldom obscured by a cloud. It means much more to the Indian village than to the English village, where a cold climate keeps the people indoors more than half the year. It is by the light of the moon that the Indian seeks his recreation.

A popular form of amusement is the play performed by strolling musicians and players. The company arrives after the harvest has been gathered, and when the villagers are idle before the sowing of the seed again. They build a temporary shed with open sides for the auditorium, and erect a stage in such a position as to catch the light of the moon as long as it lasts. The news of the arrival of the players is carried to neighbouring hamlets; and visitors come in on foot or in carts, bringing their cooking pots and preparing to make a long stay. They mean to lose nothing of the fun, and intend to see the play out to the very end. Old men and women, young children, even babies in arms, accompany the parties. The grannies bring their pet dogs, a hen or two, and possibly a few goats. They camp under some tree on the outskirts of the village, and make a picnic of their visit without fear of bad weather in their glorious climate.

The play begins at about nine o'clock at night and goes on till four in the morning. The audience sits through it with patience and good humour. If sleep overcomes an individual here and there, he remains where he is and slumbers peacefully till a round of applause from the more enthusiastic wakes him up. He loses nothing, for he has probably seen the play frequently since he was a child, and he is able to pick up the thread of the plot easily.

The acts and scenes are numerous; and it takes

two or three weeks to finish the piece. The people assemble each evening, and follow it to the end, going about their work in the day and devoting the night to the theatre. Every performance begins with the appearance of the jester, who uses the same old tricks for raising a laugh which serve the clown and pantaloon in the Christmas pantomime. The broad wit of the Bottoms and Shallows of the East is greeted with shouts of laughter, the jokes being unimpaired by either age or familiarity.

The company brings its own musicians. They are not of the same caste as the tomtom beaters who play at the devil-dance. These men have more or less studied the intricate Indian system of harmony, which includes quarter-tones as well as semi-tones, and gives the octave twenty-seven notes. They play on stringed instruments, producing thin wailing notes without much volume. To the uninitiated, Indian music is melancholy and unsatisfactory. English ears fail to recognise the quarter-tones except as discords. On the other hand, the musically educated Hindu finds the European music crude and barbaric compared with his own, and sees very little to admire in it.

On dark nights when there is no moon lamps

A HINDU MUSICIAN

He is playing on a stringed instrument, known in the south as a tambour. Musicians have a caste of their own and they are allowed to enter the courtyards of the village houses, which is forbidden to the pariah tomtom-beater and the horn-blower of the devil-dance.

are lighted; but the light is dim and casts deep shadows. Possibly this is an advantage to the players; for their tinsel and coloured cotton garments are of the most tawdry description, and show signs of careless and constant wear.

The Hindu playgoer is not critical as to the dress of the actors, who are always men; and he is totally indifferent as to scenery. His eye is easily pleased with the glitter of gold and silver lace and strings of glass beads. It is the plot that he delights in, with its extravagant emotion and romance. He revels in the adventures of Rajah Hari Chandra, his Ranee, and their noble son.

The Rajah is driven from his throne by his ungrateful subjects for maintaining truth and discountenancing duplicity. He and his Ranee, Chandra Mahdi, become separated in their wanderings, the boy following the mother. To support herself and her child the Ranee is obliged to take service in the family of a Brahman priest. She has to pound rice, grind curry-stuff, and wash the cooking pots. Her child is bitten by a snake and dies; and Chandra Mahdi's grief gives the actor a fine opportunity of showing his histrionic powers.

The body is taken to the burning ground where no less a person than the deposed Rajah is employed as custodian. As such it is his duty to cremate the corpse, a task he carries out without discovering the identity of the boy. His grief when he learns the true facts of the case is another opportunity which is made the most of by the actor.

A play as popular as Hari Chandra and given as frequently is founded on the story of Markanda. The parents of Markanda entreated Siva to give them a son. The god heard their prayer and offered them a choice between a child who should be handsome, wise and good, but only live to the age of sixteen, or a son, ugly, wicked and irreligious, who should live to be a hundred.

They chose the good son; and when he was born named him Markanda. At the age of fifteen he was told the story of his birth and its conditions, and he was informed by his parents that he had only a short time to live. He resolved to retire from the world and spend his remaining days in prayer to Siva.

The god of Death, terrible to look at, appeared at the appointed hour, riding upon a bull buffalo. He discharged his arrows of sickness, pain, and death at his victim as the boy prayed. The arrows fell harmless around Markanda and he was unhurt.

A HINDU MUSICIAN

His instrument is made of a dried gourd and a single string. He is a caste man with certain privileges in the practice of his profession.

Then the god of Death drew his sword; but before he could slay him, Siva appeared and stayed his hand. As a reward for his piety Markanda was given perpetual youth with exemption from death.

The appearance of Death thrills the audience with dread and fear. All their sympathy is roused on behalf of the saintly Markanda, and they rejoice when he escapes his fate. These two well-known dramas never fail to draw appreciative audiences. They may be crudely staged and even badly played; but the moral, the triumph of good, is never lost sight of; nor is the sympathy of the audience ever misplaced.

The villager does not always take his recreation in the dark hours of the night. There are days when work is slack and high holiday may be made with impunity. These are the occasions for cock-fights and ram- and bull-fights, against which there is no legal prohibition.

The bulls are trained to fight against men. The animals use their horns and hoofs in self-defence. Their assailants are unarmed. It frequently happens that the young men who try to capture the bulls are injured. The Indian bull, which is small, is extraordinarily quick and active in its movements. The reward of the successful bullfighter is a new loin-cloth with money tied in a corner of it. This is fastened to the horns of the bull; and it is the perquisite of any one who can lead the animal to its master. A clever bull may live to make a great reputation as it comes out of the fight unsubdued.

Ram- and cock-fighting are more cruel sports, as the creatures are pitted against each other; and they are encouraged to continue fighting long after one of the combatants has shown signs of distress and defeat. Rams will go on fighting for hours, the conqueror severely injuring the conquered before the latter will turn tail and run. It is the same with the cocks. They are sometimes armed with sharp double-edge knives as spurs with which they rend and tear each other terribly. A cock-fight can only be determined by the flight or death of the vanquished; and the owner of the victor claims the beaten bird as his reward unless some other arrangement has been made.

All Hindu villagers have their games in which the boys and young men take part. They correspond with the games played on village greens in England. There is a kind of indigenous cricket that requires no pitch—a difficult thing to provide in a sun-burned plain with no turf. The player holds both the bat and the ball. He throws the ball and strikes it high into the air for the field to catch. The boy who succeeds in making the catch claims his turn to bat.

Another popular game is a kind of prisoner's base, played with a captain on each side. The ancient art of single-stick is taught; and also wrestling. Small boys play a game with marbles, using a smooth surface much after the fashion of English boys. Tamarind seeds are used like knuckle-bones. The polished surface of the seeds make the game more difficult than with bones as the pips slip off the back of the hand more easily than bones.

Women and girls never join in the village games, nor do they go to the bull-fights. They may look on from a distance and turn admiring glances on the young men as they dance by moonlight in the village street; but there is no mixing of the sexes or joining in the active games.

The girls have a dance of their own. It is not like the nautch, and cannot rightly be called a dance, being more like the physical drill introduced into kindergarten schools. The players clap their hands or strike short rods together to keep time, as they step in unison with a bending of the body from side to side. The loose folds of the sari leave them free to move, with the result that they show a natural unconscious grace that is very attractive.

The older women play games with tamarind seeds or cowries on a chequered board marked with obstacles and penalties. They also use cupped boards, dropping the seeds in certain numerical order into the cups until the whole are accumulated into a single heap. This is called bank. Instead of cubed dice they cast the cowries and count those that fall with the bifurcated side uppermost.

Once a week the village has its market-day. In towns with a large population the market is held every day; also in places where Europeans reside like Ootacamund, Bangalore, and other stations. The market is known as "shandy."

In the Indian village up-country the market is held once a week only. Produce of all kinds is brought in, and people come from a distance to buy their weekly supplies. The commodities are laid out on mats or in baskets. If the weather is damp, temporary stalls are improvised with loose boards supported on empty kerosene tins. Space is left for the customers to walk round or even to seat themselves if they wish to enjoy a long tough haggle over quantity and price.

THE VEGETABLE MARKET AT OOTACAMUND

It is locally known as the "Shandy." The display is chiefly tomatoes, greens, oranges, carrots, etc.

A market in the Indian sunlight always presents a picturesque scene with its rich and varied colouring. In the tomato season the shandy at Ootacamund is a blaze of colour with the crimson tomatoes, the yellow oranges, limes and shaddock, the different greens of the cabbages, knol-kohl, curled kale and native vegetables, the purple of the egg-plant—the brinjal as it is called—the creamy turnips, and the brick-red carrots.

In addition to the vegetables there are other goods for sale: drapery, tin and brass ware, china and iron ware, grain of every description, stalls devoted to the sale of betel leaf, and areca nut and sweetmeats. The throng of people purchasing, or gossiping and idling, lends additional colour to the already brilliant scene. Their clothes are mostly of white, red, blue and yellow, and they are draped about their figures without much assistance from the tailor's scissors or the dressmaker's sewing machine.

A market on the hills is very attractive to the European. In the clean cool climate of the Nilgiri Hills there is no dust and no extreme heat to mar the freshness of the fruit brought in direct from the gardens where it is grown. In the village of the plains the picturesqueness barely compensates the visitor for the heat he has to endure, the dust, the swarm of flies, and various other discomforts, including the fear of infection.

In the village market payments are often made in kind. For so much grain delivered by the cultivator he is allowed to take a certain amount of goods from the shopkeeper. If an individual is employed by Government he receives his salary in rupees. He pays the greater part over to the tradesman, and draws supplies as long as his credit lasts.

The same system prevails among the servants of the English. The shopkeeper attends the different houses on the day when the wages are paid, and three-fourths of the money is placed in his hands. The system has its advantages; food supplies—rice and curry stuffs—never run short; but it also has its disadvantages. The servants are entirely at the mercy of the tradesman, and they are obliged to take the goods he offers at any charge he may choose to make. Fortunately for them he is content with a moderate profit as a rule, and is not so rapacious as the money-lender whose exorbitancy hardly knows a limit.

The system of cash payments, such as has come into vogue in the West with the foundation of large

A HINDU MUSICIAN WITH A CYMBAL USED WITH THE STRINGED INSTRUMENTS

The cymbal is beaten like a drum with the finger ends and with the lower part of the palm. Two notes are thus produced and they are varied by the clash of the metal discs.

stores, is unknown except in a few of the most important towns of India where there is a community of Europeans and Eurasians. It would not answer in the Indian village for the simple reason that there is little or no money in circulation. The people prefer to follow in the footsteps of their ancestors and make payments in kind, either in produce or labour. It would be inadvisable to alter existing conditions. The villager is a child in the matter of keeping money. He might be able to hide it in a hole under his floor and leave it untouched; but to spend it slowly and by degrees on legitimate necessities for his household would be beyond his powers.

The village system is as firmly rooted in the land as the family system and the caste system. The people are contented with it and desire no change. It is useless to talk of progress and improvement. Rules of life that governed their fathers are good enough for them. On the other hand they are quite ready to adopt improved tools and European machinery. When the sewing machine made its first appearance among the tailors they believed the rapid and regular stitching could only be the work of a devil shut in the box and they did pujah to it. Now the sewing machine is part of the tailor's outfit, as necessary as his needle and thread.

Another article that has been adopted throughout the whole of India is mineral oil as a lighting medium. No village, however remote and secluded, is without its cheap little paraffin lamp. It has superseded the safer but less illuminating vegetable oils ; and it is often the cause of disastrous fires. Though the people may be ready to benefit by importations of this kind, they would resent the abolition of their village headman, their panchelar, their sweeper, barber, dhoby, or their punchayet. Outside their own home-rule system they know nothing and care less. They understand nothing about party politics and its aim. Bishop Caldwell related that when he was travelling among the hills of South India he came across some men belonging to a jungle tribe who were not aware that the British authority was established throughout the land. They believed that they were still living under the Pandian kings. When asked to account for the presence of the European in India they said that they thought he was there for his own amusement to hunt the wild beasts of the forest.

An educated native was asked if he thought

that the villagers were satisfied with the rule of the British Government. The reply was to the following effect:

"The English respect our caste and our village institutions, and they give us religious liberty and local self-government in our punchayets. Could we look with any certainty for similar concessions from any other nation, European or Asiatic?"

THE NILGIRI HILLS

Say not that all these creeds are false,
The false ones capture hearts by the scent of truth.
Say not they are all erroneous thoughts,
There is thought in the world void of reality,
He who says everything is true is a fool,
He who says all is false is a knave.

Masnawi (translated by WHINFIELD).

CHAPTER XIV

THE NILGIRI HILLS

THE Madras Presidency is not made up entirely of scorching plains where dust-storms blow and devils ride the whirlwind in the hot season; and where vegetation springs into leaf and bud under warm torrential downpour in the rainy season. It has its hills and plateau land easily accessible to the European who revels in a subtropical climate rivalling the sunny slopes of Sicily.

The Nilgiri Hills form part of the Western Ghats and lie south of the Mysore plateau. For years they were seen from a distance by the Englishmen, a line of mysterious ethereal blue like a serrated wall of forest. Those who approached found them pathless and repellent, too vast, too impenetrable to invite the explorer, who was bound to the plains by his duty to his employer, the old John Company.

It was not until the year 1800 that they were

invaded by a European. Dr. Francis Buchanan, following the tracks used by the native hill people, climbed up from the Bowani valley. He was not in search of a climate, nor had he any thought of a sanatorium for his fellow-men. His object was mineral and vegetable products that might be turned to account in the enormous market that the Company had created during the last two hundred years. Gold, silver, iron, diamonds, timber, gall-nuts, ebony, sandalwood; anything, in short, that could be dealt with commercially.

What he found was of inestimable value, although it could not be sent home to be sold with the spices of the East. It was the *soma*, the nectar of the Indian gods, the life-restoring breezes of the hill-tops that have often robbed death of its prey during the last hundred years.

It was not until 1818 that his discovery could be exploited. In that year Kindersley and Whish, of the Company's civil service, set out on a shooting expedition with Buchanan's El Dorado as their goal. They took the same route by way of the Bowani River valley. The track was not very promising, but they had Buchanan's report to encourage them to persevere. They passed through the dry thorny zone of scrubby deciduous jungle

A MAN BELONGING TO ONE OF THE FOREST TRIBES OF THE WESTERN GHATS

These men possess a wonderful knowledge of the jungle and the game that is to be found. Round his arm is an amulet to protect him from accidents. He served as a beater, and entered the forest with his companions unarmed to turn out a tiger. They are said to possess a knowledge of magic. It is quite certain that they have some knowledge of the use of hypnotism; but it is not sufficient to render them immune from accident.

which falls an easy prey to the forest fire. Gradually, as they mounted, the bamboos grew less dense; the cactus and then the palm disappeared, and they entered the fairy land of fern, perennial evergreen, and the giant forest tree. They came upon bud and blossom. The cool air blew down from crag and moorland above with the revivifying effect of champagne. They emerged on the downs above the spot where Ootacamund now stands, and with their advent the Englishman had at last "come to stay."

At that time it was the custom for those in the Company's service whose health had failed to take a trip to the Cape for change of air. The two men recognised the fact that here, close at hand, was a better sanatorium than the coast of South Africa could offer. Here was a spot that might be reached, if roads were opened, in as many hours as it took days to get to Cape Town. Here the delicate drooping children and fading wives might be brought to recuperate their strength with little trouble and small expense.

They returned full of their discovery and communicated their enthusiasm to John Sullivan who was in the same service as themselves. He was "Collector" of Coimbatore, a district adjoining the Nilgiris, and he lost no time in following the footsteps of Kindersley and Whish. He found that their story was not exaggerated; and he at once threw himself heart and soul into the suggested sanatorium scheme. The mountain paths were opened up and the plateau made more accessible. He built the first house, and was, in fact, the father of Ootacamund and Coonoor.

Stephen Lushington, Governor of Madras between 1827 and 1830, lent himself to the scheme, and under his governorship the Nilgiris became the recognised hill resort of the Presidency.

In those days the journey had to be done chiefly by human transport through the aid of the local hillmen, assisted by Lumbadis, the wandering Indian Gipsies who for centuries have been the recognised carriers of the Western Ghats. Later a cart-road was made; and the beginning of the twentieth century saw the road superseded by the railway.

The beauty of the evergreen forests, with their noble trees, their flowering shrubs and variety of fern, is very striking. The giants rise on single massive stems to a height of eighty feet or more, bearing compact crowns of foliage except where they stand on the border of the grass lands. There they extend long arms thickly clothed with glossy leaves, the favourite haunt of the sun-loving birds and butterflies. Underneath the forest tree is an undergrowth rising in the "chequered" shade some thirty feet—tree-ferns, wild laurel, crimson rhododendron, the purple osbeckia, bramble, wild guava, and other flowering and fruiting shrubs. Beneath these again is yet another luxuriant growth where the sun never penetrates. The moist, soft leaf-mould lying between the boulders of the steep slopes is covered with moss and fern and lycopodiums such as are only seen in a hot-house in the temperate zone.

The blackwood of the Western Ghats is said to be the ebony of the ancients of which they built their war chariots. So wonderful was it in its resistance to attack that the old warriors worshipped their chariots as being god-given and supernaturally endowed. A very handsome tree is the teak with its large leaf and vivid greens; but the most beautiful at the coming of the rains is the ironwood, which sends up its shoots a blood-red crimson, turning the blue of the hills to a rich purple.

A striking feature of all tropical forests that are evergreen are the insidious creepers, so tender and fragile in youth, so tenacious and death-dealing in old age. Some of them are armed with thorns and some with tendrils, but they hang and cling with their bodies like snakes, and there is no escape from their grip when once the embrace has been made. Their length is incredible, and there is no height they cannot reach. They possess an unerring instinct in their search for support, bending against all the laws of gravitation towards the strong young limbs of the tree near by, as if the plant possessed some mysterious volition of its own. The age of the creeper is said to be greater than that of the tree. It is certain that many of the giants may be found dead in their arms, the tough jungle-rope of nature curiously twined and twisted to the very top, and the foliage of the parasite replacing the foliage of the tree. The natives say that these weird climbing plants are vivified with the souls of treacherous human beings, who continue their perfidious lives in the vegetable world, drawing the life-blood from others that they themselves may flourish.

There is a climber in the Ceylon forests which has been nicknamed by the planters "The Agent" (the money-lender or the sowcar). The tree that supports it slowly withers and dies whilst the creeper flourishes, an example of how the sowcar benefits by the planter's labour.

The word forest conjures up to the English mind visions of green glades and pleasant grassy slopes, ideal spots whereon to picnic and pitch the holiday camp. The Indian forest offers nothing of the kind. There are no glades and grassy banks. It is dense and impenetrable except by game tracks and narrow, tortuous paths scarcely discernible to the inexperienced eye. The tracks run parallel with the ridges above or the valleys below, turning here and there to reach a water pool or to cross to another hill.

To step off these tracks is to plunge at once into dense vegetation. The beds of fern and moss beneath the undergrowth cover hidden stones and the rocky beds of mountain runlets. Progress is arrested by formidable thorns; and at every point of the compass a wall of foliage hems in the adventurous traveller. It is impossible to see the sun or to feel the direction of the wind which cannot penetrate below the roof of foliage. The forest becomes one vast bed of vegetation deprived of all its distinguishing marks.

There is nothing more paralysing to the human

being than to be lost in the jungle. It holds the wanderer under a spell of helpless confusion, with an increasing sensation of bewilderment at every step. It seems as though the forest itself becomes inimical and hostile towards the intruder. While he keeps to the path he is regarded with a tolerant smile; but now he offends, he is trespassing. Advance is made in the teeth of opposition. The ground that looks so smooth has holes and unexpected pitfalls hidden beneath that bed of fern. The brambles and rattans cling tenaciously, wounding as they grip; and the more the axe is used to cut away the undergrowth the thicker the jungle appears to be. To add to the trouble there is a stifling sensation in the stagnant air which no breeze, however strongly it may be blowing above the tree-tops, can reach at that depth of the forest.

The traveller stops and listens with a firm determination to keep his head. The jungle is strangely silent, yet it seems to have a thousand eyes that watch and mock at him in his difficulties. Birds cease twittering, or they utter warning croaks, and every wild animal within scent lies low in dread of man. If he has a rifle, his best plan is to fire it, and then call for help.

In answer there may come an old man of the

Kurumba caste such as may be seen in the picture. Born like the leopard and the monkey in the forest, he knows every track as the lost man knows his own garden. With his knife he hacks a passage through the undergrowth to the stranger. His deep-set eyes glance to right and left, and then he leads the way back to the lost path and civilisation.

These men serve as shikarees in the Nilgiri hills and in the forests of Mysore. They find the game for the English sportsman, and go into the jungle unarmed to beat it out. They are a strange race, with a knowledge of hypnotism and a firm belief in magic and witchcraft. The natives fear them as magicians with a supernatural power over animals. The Canarese credit them with the power of stopping a charging beast, even to the extent of making a tiger lie down, at the word of command, by the side of a herd of cattle. Their services are in great request for the practice of magic, the driving away of evil spirits and averting the malice of devils that haunt trees, streams, and rocks. If the crops are devastated by wild animals, the Kurumba is sent for to trap and kill, and lay a spell on the field that shall keep off the intruders. There is a story that an old

Kurumba attempted by repeating spells to stop and turn away a mischievous elephant that was wrecking a field of sugar-cane in Mysore. The animal, however, paid no attention to the muntrams, but charged the magician, who fled before him like a cat from an express train and took refuge in a tree.

The Kurumbas have many strange beliefs about the wild animals themselves. Every member of the tribe is said to have his affinity in the forest, his animal brother who will do him no harm. It may be a bear, a monkey, a deer, or one of the feline species, or it may be a bird or reptile. He will know his brother by intuition and by the frequency with which the animal will dog his steps. They also believe in the were-tiger and were-leopard, creatures whose bodies are the abode of men of evil passions. Through the agency of the tiger or panther these human beings are able to indulge their passions without restraint. Supernaturally endowed beasts are believed to be safe from the shikaree's ordinary weapons; their human cunning enables them to avoid the traps and pitfalls set for them, and no ordinary leaden bullet can harm them. Nothing but a specially prepared lethal weapon is of any use, a bullet or a knife

A HINDU, PROBABLY OF THE BIRD-TRAPPER TRIBE

He is a well-known figure in Madras where he sells bows and clay balls, used by servants to shoot at thieving crows in the verandahs. His bow has a double string. The pellet is in his closed hand ready to be discharged.

over which pujah has been performed. When the animal is at last wounded, or perhaps killed outright, the man who has made use of its body mysteriously sickens or dies.

How far the Kurumba pulls the strings to bring about his desired results it is impossible to say. There is no doubt that his hypnotic power, combined with fear on the part of the credulous native, is sufficient to cause sickness or even death. The oriental imagination lends assistance in producing mysterious effects in the East.

The Kurumba possesses marvellous skill in tracking. His eye detects signs where the inexperienced can see nothing. A kick given to the soil, the pressure of the grass, the trail of a small piece of bamboo or a creeping plant are sufficient for him to determine the direction in which the animal is travelling and the time that has elapsed since it passed. It is for this reason and for his intimate knowledge of the forest that he is so much in request as a shikaree and beater when big game is hunted. He has little fear of death because he believes that he can avoid it. Now and then, however, a beater is killed by a wounded tiger in spite of covering rifles. His faith is pinned to the amulet that he ties round his arm. It may contain the whiskers of a particularly dangerous panther or tiger killed by a spear on which a spell had been laid, or the claw of a were-leopard that no trap or pitfall could take. The old man in the picture is wearing a charm round the arm above the elbow.

Their religion is animistic. They worship the spirits of the forests, using blood sacrifices in their pujah. In the days before British rule they probably offered human beings to their gods. A human sacrifice is now treated as a murder; if attempted without the co-operation of others, it is treated as suicide.

An old man very similar to the one here pictured threw himself before the wheels of the motor car in which Sir Arthur and Lady Lawley were driving when on tour through the district. Fortunately they were proceeding at a slow pace at the time on account of the crowd that lined the road, and the projected sacrifice was prevented. No explanation was given by the man for his action, nor by the crowd, assembled probably to see it. They were satisfied, no doubt, that the attempt had been made; and if the God of the English Governor chose to avert it, the will must be taken for the deed by the spirits of the forest.

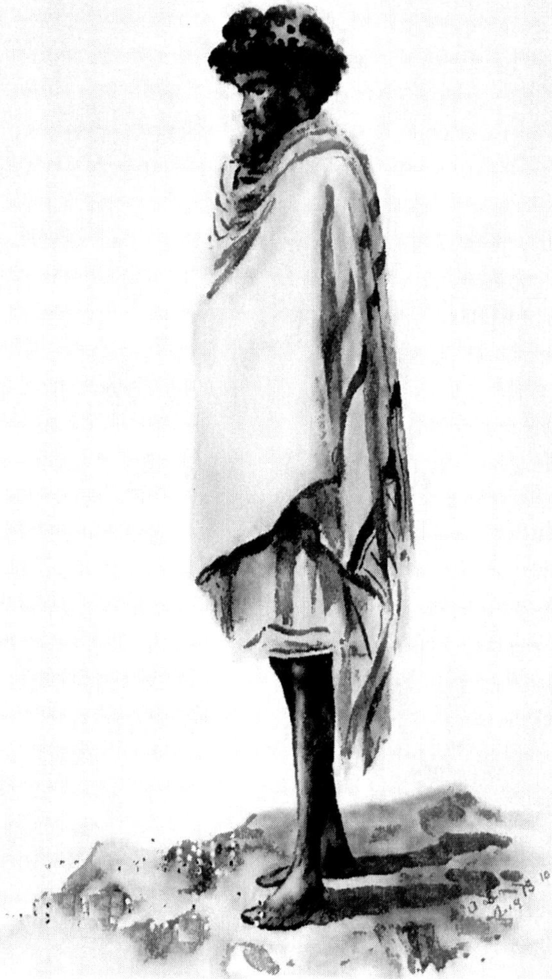

A MAN BELONGING TO THE TODA TRIBE, NILGIRI HILLS

The Todas are herdsmen and own a race of semi-wild buffaloes with hairy coats and curved serrated horns. Polyandry is practised among the Todas, the brothers of the same family possessing one wife in common. The brothers remain at home in turn to protect the woman and her children while the rest are out pasturing their cattle on the hills. Their dwellings are made of bent sticks matted over with palm-leaf mats or thatched with boughs.

When the Kurumba is not employed in hunting or performing magic he cuts firewood, gathers honey, and collects other produce of the forest for which there is a sale in the agricultural villages. He also makes an excellent woodman in the service of the Government Forest Department.

In addition to the Kurumbas and other forest tribes there exists on the Nilgiris a strange race of aboriginals known as the Todas. They are of dark complexion with curly hair. They wear no turban or cap. A blanket of local manufacture serves as dress. It is draped over their bodies, and its rough surface sheds the raindrops like the coat of an animal.

Their marriage customs have brought them a kind of notoriety, as they practise polyandry. The brothers of a family share a wife between them. Only one brother remains at home. The rest go out with their herds of buffaloes to pasture them in the distant valleys where grass is plentiful. They take it by turn to stay at home with the woman and her children, and under this system no difficulties occur of choice or favour.

They are a pastoral people avoiding the forests and keeping to the grassy slopes with their buffaloes, a fine race of their kind. The buffaloes are covered with long brown hair, and they possess formidable horns of great length, serrated like the horns of an ibex. They have a peculiar aversion to horses, and will attack and gore them unprovoked, placing the rider in considerable danger. A Toda boy will exercise a wonderful control over the half-wild animals. Armed with small jagged bits of rock which he can throw with excellent aim, he will drive a herd away from the path and keep the bulls in check. The danger is lest the imp should be asleep or out of the way when his services are required.

The Todas live in huts formed of wickerwork, covered with a thatch of some kind, and their villages are called munds. They are more of the nature of encampments than permanent hamlets. The entrance to the hut is very low, and the owners have to enter on their hands and knees. There are no windows, and the interior is dark. In or near every mund is a tree that is held sacred to the deity. There used to be a tree preserved in the barrack square at Wellington near Coonoor, the military sanatorium of the Nilgiris. It was surrounded with masonry, and occasionally the Todas came to do pujah underneath it. It was removed some years ago to make room for the manœuvres of the troops in the square.

Once a year the Todas foregather for the purpose of propitiating a mysterious deity to whom they offer a buffalo. The system of killing the beast was cruel. It was driven through a narrow opening, and the young men armed with knives made cuts at it as it passed, rarely dealing it a death-blow. The animal lingered in a maimed condition for some hours, perhaps days. The method was prohibited by Government, and it was ordered that the buffalo should be killed outright.

The Toda is not an artisan nor an agriculturalist, and he stands out in strong contrast to the Budaga and the Kota, the latter being the artisan of the Western Ghats. The Budaga is as industrious as the Toda is idle. Industry and an innate love of order are his characteristics. He builds himself a neat house with mud walls and tiled or thatched roof. His patience in tilling the ground is remarkable. It is not a smooth field of rich soil that he deals with, but a sloping, uneven surface covered with boulders of every size and shape. Instead of a plough he uses a pick, and what soil there is between the boulders he turns over and levels as best he can to receive the seed. He is dependent on showers for irrigation, and there are seasons when these fail and all his labour is of no avail. Still he perseveres, putting in nothing but hand labour of the severest kind.

The Budaga continues to pay a small tribute to the Toda, which, however, the Toda cannot legally enforce. Possibly the payment is made with the understanding that the crops will be protected from trespass on the part of the Todas' cattle.

The language of the Budagas is akin to Malayalam, but the origin of the race is not known. He is of fairer complexion than the Toda, who is swarthy, and the Kurumba, who is dark brown. He is not known to exist anywhere except on the Nilgiri Hills. There is not much crime among these peaceful hill tribes. The Budagas are too busy, the Todas and Kurumbas are too remote from their fellow-men to suffer much from friction with other races.

The Budagas worship local deities. They are visited occasionally by gurus or religious teachers whom they reverence. When a visit is under contemplation word is sent that the guru is coming. The Budagas turn out in numbers to

A MAN OF THE BUDAGA CASTE

A cultivator on the Nilgiri hills and to be found nowhere else. He is more civilised than the Toda, to whom he pays a small tax for the privilege of growing his corn and vegetables. His house is built of sun-dried bricks, tiled or thatched. His turban of unbleached calico is always neatly folded, a mark of his innate love of tidiness. The Budagas are an industrious race of law-abiding agriculturists, whose worst enemy is the uncertain monsoon. They depend entirely on the local rainfall.

meet him, marching in single line along the mountain paths, chanting as they go. The sound of the melancholy musical notes sung by a file of men more than half-a-mile long has a curious effect in the echoing valleys, or on the hill-tops as they mount a shoulder and disappear on the other side.

They have a tradition that ages ago the Nilgiris were inhabited by a race of white giants, whose spirits may still be seen on moonlight nights, flitting up the lonely gorges and on the rocky slopes of Dodabetta, the highest mountain of the range. The belief in old-time giants is not peculiar to the Budagas. It lingers on the plains and on the plateau, wherever boulders are to be found. Ignorant of the power of cold and heat and of erosion by water, the oriental has no other way of explaining the presence of the boulder and the strange position in which it is often left, balanced on the top of a crag or poised on the hillside, except by the belief that it was thrown there. The giants warred with the gods or with themselves and used the boulders as missiles. The only other solution of gigantic stones being found on the slopes of mountains and on the plains is in the fable recorded in the *Arabian Nights Tales.*

They are the petrified princes who, with their horses and suites, were turned to stone for presumptuously aspiring to the hand of a beautiful princess—a fancy that is alluring though no longer credible except in the romantic East.

A CANARESE WATER WOMAN

The panniers are made of bamboo. The mouths of the brass pots are stuffed with green leaves to prevent the water from slopping over as the bullock walks.

THE GUM TREE AND THE FOREST

It is prudent to live on good terms with one's cook, with ballad-mongers, with doctors, with magicians, with the ruler of one's country, with rich people, and with obstinate folk.

Niti Sloka, xliii. (DUBOIS).

A CANARESE WOMAN

The Canarese affect blue in all shades. Their saris are bordered with a beautiful shade of gold-green colour in which runs a thread of dark red. Lady Lawley says: "This woman worked in the Government House garden at Ootacamund. I had great difficulty in persuading my peon to call her to stand for me. In his opinion she was not a fit model for 'an Excellency' to paint. I had the same difficulty with all my low-caste models at first. After every effort on the part of my two peons to make me realise that I ought not to allow low-caste people to approach me, they resigned themselves to my odd taste in old and dirty effects. They proved themselves very clever in bringing me most artistic models regardless of caste."

CHAPTER XV

THE GUM TREE AND THE FOREST

THE hill tribes are of no use in the gardens of Ootacamund and Coonoor. They can fell trees and cut down jungle; perhaps put up a garden fence; but there their utility ends, and the lover of flowers must look to another race to tend his roses and picotees, his geraniums and heliotrope, his dahlias and tuberoses. The Canarese, the agriculturist of Mysore and the plateaus of the Western Ghat, is the man he must turn to for the care of his flower-beds. The work of weeding and watering is congenial to the Canarese, and both men and women follow the calling of Adam *con amore.*

The old woman with the basket on her head has spent the whole of her life among the flowers in the Government House gardens at Ootacamund. In her dark indigo sari, with its broad border of yellow green, she is in colour harmony with the mimosa that scents the air. Like one of the creatures of the forest she moves noiselessly and goes through her task without haste, cleaning paths, weeding beds and borders, removing dead leaves and sticks and tidying up after the pruner. She is in keeping with the green barbets and grey babblers that haunt the grevillia trees and rose hedges, and with the green and black butterflies and metallic honey-suckers that rob the fuchsia bells.

The mimosa was introduced with the eucalyptus from Australia in the middle of the nineteenth century, and it flourishes exceedingly, bidding fair to become a pest like the lantana. A Revenue Official of the Nilgiris named Thomas planted numbers of blue gums as well as black gums (the Acacia melanoxylon) and the wattle. The gums have grown into large forest trees, and they have given Ootacamund the appearance of having been built in a forest. When the place was first opened up by Sullivan the site was little better than a bog. It was bare of trees except for small sholas in the moist valleys. Now the place is thickly wooded with the evergreen gum.

The eucalyptus and the melanoxylon have a sombre and distinct beauty of their own; the one a dark heavy green, the other almost grey in the brilliant sunlight. In its early growth the eucalyptus clothes itself in a tender foliage of emerald bloom. When it reaches maturity it loses the round leaf and assumes a tough scimitar-shaped foliage not unlike that of the English willow. The trunk, tall and straight, sheds its bark in long ragged streamers that sway in the wind and give the tree an appearance of decay it is far from experiencing. Wood, bark, seeds, and foliage are strongly impregnated with the pungent oil which is now an article of commerce in South India. Neither fern nor shrub will grow beneath the tree, a fact that alters the character of the eucalyptus forest and makes it entirely different from the indigenous shola.

The native calls it the firewood tree, as every part of it will burn green. The frayed ribbons of bark constantly falling from its stem, together with the dry leathery leaves, form a perennial harvest to the wood-gatherer. The grass-cutter —the syce's wife or mother—relies upon it for the boiling of the horse-gram.

The woman in the sketch has been gleaning for the stable as well as for herself; for in addition to cutting grass and preparing the gram for the horse she has to cook for the syce and his children. She looks cold, poor soul! in the chill evening air of the mountains. In appearance she is not unlike the friendly firewood tree, with her ragged old sari hanging in ribbons, and her unkempt hair blowing about in the wind. The sharp hill breeze that brings health and strength to the Englishman nips her and leaves her shrivelled. Every day, rain or sun, she must go out in search of the tale of grass and the bundle of firewood.

The master gives the syce a liberal allowance to buy wood, but, after the manner of his kind, the horsekeeper prefers to spend the money on beer and arrack in the shandy; and he leaves his mother-in-law or his wife to provide fuel as she can. The children help to boil the gram; and when grannie is not looking, the little black fists are dipped into the gram-pot, and the pug noses buried in the warm gram. The boys do not feel the cold like the old woman; and life for them even away from the sun-burned village of the plains is full of pleasure. The grannie's happiest moments are those, when wrapped in an ancient horse-jhool, she has stowed herself away in the warmest corner of the stable, a shapeless human bundle, on an armful of straw—stolen like the jhool and the gram from the horse.

A TAMIL PARIAH WOMAN, ONE OF THE DESPISED OUTCASTES

She has gathered branches of the cucalyptus to burn, the firewood tree, as the natives call it, because it burns green. The blue gums were introduced into the hills of South India from Australia. They have flourished and have reclothed some of the hill-sides, deforested by charcoal burners before the forests were protected.

A little later the stable will be empty. The syce, no longer tempted by the overweening delights of the tavern in the shandy, will become the soberest of grooms; and the little party will be met going down the ghat road; the syce well-clothed, well-beturbaned and empty-handed, leading the horse; the children wearily yet happily plodding over the metalled road with bare feet, each carrying a bundle; and grannie bringing up the rear in company with an elderly coolie woman, each staggering under a load of stable properties, and with difficulty keeping up with the lord and master in front. The bark of the gum trees will fall to the ground unheeded for a time, making a rich store for the next season.

The gums have helped to drain the basin of the settlement; and the stream that wandered through the bog has been embanked and turned into a beautiful lake. The grassy banks that slope upwards from the sheet of water are tufted with rushes and set with wild balsams. The balsam has two creamy petals dotted with a tiny purple eye, and the stamens are hidden in a slender curved horn. The pink orchis, purple verbena, and yellow celandine abound.

Morning and evening the soft effect of mist,

with the reds and golds of the sky, turn the lake into a fairy mirror, which reflects back the wooded landscape. The glassy surface is only broken when some water bird swims across, leaving two long trails of silver ripples flowing away from its breast at right angles.

A road runs from the end of the lake up the slope, where grows the familiar yellow gorse, and passes to the downs for which Ootacamund is famous. These downs stretch away to the north-west over miles of undulating plateau. The grass that clothes them takes a velvety sheen, making them appear smoother than they are in reality; and the air blows over them with a keenness suggestive of a Scotch moor. It is here that the hounds give the visitors to Ooty many a good run. The jackal has to serve as fox as a rule, and he makes excellent sport. There is a grey fox with a black tip to its tail which is occasionally killed, but the jack is more common and equally game.

To the north-west of Ootacamund beyond the downs lie the Kundah Hills, also part of the Western Ghats. The higher portion of the range is covered with grass; but in every valley and cleft is to be found the thick shola of stunted,

EARLY MORNING ON THE LAKE, OOTA-
CAMUND, WITH MIST RISING

weather-beaten trees that nestle away from the winds and give shelter to the big game. Sambur, ibex, jungle-sheep, bison, and elephants still survive the trapping of the forest tribes; and the prowling tiger and panther wander from cover to cover.

To the south beyond Coonoor and on the very outskirts of the Nilgiris lies the Hoolicul Droog, a noble mountain mass at the entrance of the pass up which the railroad runs. On the other side it forms the wild beautiful valley of the Bowani River. The Droog, a term derived from *durga*, a fort, is like a crouching lion. Its lower slopes have been cleared in places for coffee and tea plantations. The head of the mountain rises in cliffs of grey rock, as perpendicular and inaccessible as the walls of a gigantic mediæval castle. Virgin forest, untouched by the destructive charcoal burner, clings to the clefts and shelves and gorges wherever there is foothold. At the coming of the rains the iron-wood trees send out crimson shoots of fresh leaves, and the Droog is clothed with a mantle of royal purple.

On the top of the hill are the ruins of an old fort. Here Haider Ali and his son Tippu Sultan are said to have imprisoned some Englishmen taken in the Mysore wars. The fort is mentioned by Meadows Taylor in his novel, *Ralph Darnell*, the hero of which was sent there by Haider. Near it is a precipice of sheer rock. These two tyrannical Mysore usurpers caused their unfortunate native prisoners to be thrown over this and similar precipices elsewhere. The fall did not always kill the victims. They were left maimed and helpless to become a prey to the wild beasts of the forest.

The jungle that covers the back of the Droog is primeval and unexplored by man. In the remote past it is probable that the sides of Dodabetta were once similarly clothed. The difficult approach to the Droog, with its perpendicular cliffs and steep slopes, has kept the charcoal burner at bay. In these days the forest is strictly preserved; but the fear of the forest officer with the law behind him cannot altogether check the destructive hand of the native.

It is only above a certain height that the forest remains evergreen. Below that line the foliage is deciduous. During the hot season, when no rain falls for three months, the trees drop their leaves; the undergrowth becomes sear and dry; the sap goes down, and nature takes a rest.

Then is the opportunity of the forest incendiary.

He fires the dry vegetation that he may have spaces for planting a little corn and for a patch or two of fresh grass for his cattle. The ground only serves for one year, or two at most. Then the jungle takes possession, a mean thorny jungle that cannot boast of a single tree worthy of the name, and that can only offer a prolific crop of thorns.

The forest alight is a terrible thing to see. The flames lick up the vegetation, leaping twenty to thirty feet high. They devour everything, leaving behind a wilderness of black and grey ash. The bamboos explode like guns. Dead leaves and twigs whirl madly on the draught caused by the flames, and red-hot ashes shoot upwards in showers of sparks to spread the mischief.

More terrible still is the headlong race of the living creatures flying for their lives before that roaring, crackling, snapping fire. Adversity brings them into strange company. Their individual animosities are forgotten as they huddle together, jostling each other in their frantic haste to escape. The snake trodden underfoot by the monkey has no time to turn and bury his fangs in the soft flesh. The tiger has no thought to kill the deer that scatters the soil from its hoofs in his face. Breathless, straining every nerve they breast the hill together. There is no circling round or doubling back. On, on they must go; and woe betide those who find themselves brought to a standstill by a wall of rock or a chaotic group of gigantic boulders or a tangled maze of thorny creepers and brambles. Sometimes the track they are following turns downwards and leads them round in the direction of the fire. Destruction is then close at hand. They cannot see the devourer, but they can hear its roar; and the sky is blackened by volumes of murky smoke that turns the sun red and darkens the forest. If it is night the flames redden the heavens and star them with angry sparks.

Then when the fleetest and strongest of foot of that terrified crowd have reached the desired ridge, looking for safety on the other side, they may be met with a second red line that is creeping up the hill to join hands with the fire behind them. No chance to gain the banks of the river at the bottom of the valley; there is no way of escape. The flames leap upon them, scorching, blistering, and slaying, offering up to Agni, the Hindu god of fire, a holocaust of "forest folk."

Seen from the plains the forest fire is a long thin red line, ever working its way upwards along the length of the range. It extends for many miles without a break, now blazing high where it finds fuel, now dying down where it has only grass to feed it, but never expiring till it has reached its furthest limit.

MYSORE AND SERINGAPATAM

Great rivers, shady trees, medicinal plants, and virtuous people are not born for themselves, but for the good of mankind in general.

Niti Sloka, lvi. (Dubois).

A TANK IN MYSORE WITH CANARESE WOMEN DRAWING WATER

The hills in the distance are covered with thick, impenetrable jungle. The open plateau land is fertile and is cultivated or used as pasture.

CHAPTER XVI

MYSORE AND SERINGAPATAM

To the north of the Nilgiri district lies the plateau of Mysore. It is the Eden of South India; there is no other country like it with its undulating stretches of park and forest, its fertile fields of corn, its gardens and plantations. The tableland varies in height from two to three thousand feet. The ranges of mountains that run through the plateau rise to five thousand feet. Here and there are isolated rocky hills that at some distant time in the past have been crowned with forts. They are called droogs, the term being attached to some personal or place name like the Hoolicul Droog.

The builders of those forts were past masters in their art. So perfectly was each stone dressed that it fitted into its place without the aid of mortar. The sides that were turned to the exterior or interior were left rough-hewn, but the surfaces that joined were so cleverly dressed that neither air nor water could penetrate through the wall when it was finished. The stone used was granite or gneiss that did not admit of sawing, and the dressing was done by hand with a primitive tool.

The grey gneiss crops out of the ground all over the plateau. The masons quarry it in a rude fashion, but with fair accuracy, with the help of fire and water. The stone cakes off into even slabs capable of being split up into various shapes and sizes. In the towns on the plateau stone often takes the place of wooden posts and beams for verandahs and roofs; and the thinner slabs are used for tiling.

The soil of Mysore is extremely fertile, and the country is well watered. The good pasturage has produced a fine breed of white cattle used for draught purposes throughout the south of India and also in the Deccan. In the sketch of the waterwoman a bullock is bearing panniers containing pots of water. Its long horns and deep dewlap show it to be one of the Mysore breed. The woman, a Canarese, has stuffed the mouths of her pots with green leaves to prevent the water from slopping over as the animal walks.

The picture of the oil-cart gives a pair of

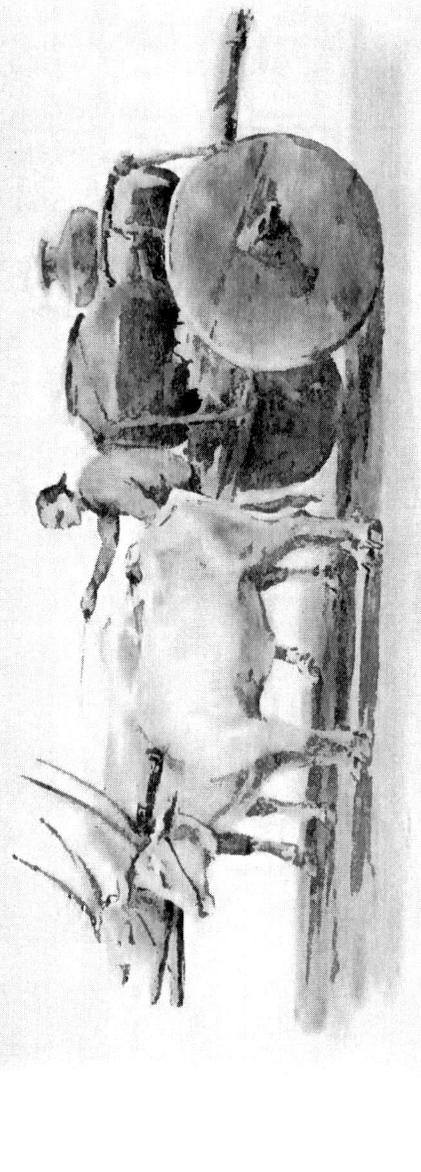

A PRIMITIVE WATER CART OF MYSORE

The wheels are of solid wood, durable but clumsy and heavy, making it very hard on the cattle to draw their loads over roads that are muddy in the rains and deep in dust during the dry season.

Mysore bullocks. The cart itself is interesting as being of the old primitive pattern in use long before the creaking of wheels was heard in England. The pattern has survived and still finds favour up country. The wheels are of solid wood, admirably adapted to the rough roads and cross-country tracks of bygone days. The capacity of the cart is small; but even so the load is often too much for the patient plodding beasts when they are required to draw it over flooded land or through the sandy bed of a dry river. The pots in the cart are filled with oil expressed in mills of equally early pattern. Every village has two or three of these mills. A block of wood revolves in a cup-shaped hollow. The seed is thrown in and the oil runs out through tiny holes in the cup. The motive power is a bullock, too often a worn-out old animal that has earned a better fate.

The history of Mysore is full of romance. The state has ever been an object of envy to northern princes who, coming from the sun-burned plains north and south of the Vindhya mountains, have looked upon it as a Paradise, and desired its equable climate and pasturage, its fruit and corn, and the gold that from remote ages has been found. One after another they conquered the peaceful agriculturists and sat down to enjoy nature's bounties; but they were not left long in peace. A fresh invading race came to rob them of their possessions which a life of luxury and ease unfitted them to defend.

The fame of Mysore reached the ears of the Muhammadan rulers of Delhi, and in A.D. 1310 a large Musalman army came south raiding and pillaging, burning and destroying as they marched. Their loot was fabulous, and they went back laden with gold and jewels.

In time the country revived and its prosperity returned. This time its splendour centred at Vijayanagar, the seat of government of the Hindu kings. Again the cupidity of the northern Muhammadans was excited by tales of the magnificence of the capital. They gathered another big army and descended on the unfortunate state, sacked Vijayanagar, and broke up the last of the Hindu Kingdoms of Mysore.

The state, which was of much greater extent than in the present day, was divided among vassal chiefs who swore fealty to the Moghul. One of these was Shahji, a Mahratta, the father of the famous Sivaji. Through him a Mahratta element was introduced, and it spread to the plains as far as Tanjore, where the fair-complexioned handsome men and women of the town still attract attention. They are the descendants of the fighting men who accompanied Shahji and afterwards attached themselves to the fortunes of his son. The girl in the sketch belongs to one of these Mahratta families. She wears a handsome silk sari bordered with gold, and holds in her hands a wreath of marigold flowers. The Mahrattas preserve their traditions and are proud of their birth, holding the dark people among whom they live in no little contempt.

The career of Sivaji was full of adventure. He threw off allegiance to the Moghul, quarrelled with the Moghul's generals, and became a law unto himself, a freebooter, like so many of the chiefs and naicks of that period. The Hindus have of recent years exalted him into a patriotic hero because he shook off the yoke of the Muhammadans; but at the time this was not the view taken by those who suffered from the raids of his marauding horsemen.

For some time Mysore remained in an unsettled state, without a ruler strong enough to take a definite lead and deliver the people from the bands of robbers whose presence paralysed agriculture and trade.

In the middle of the eighteenth century a Muhammadan trooper of an irregular corps attracted the attention of the Hindu minister, who was trying without much success to establish his sovereign's authority. The minister had noted his personal courage and military skill. He promoted him and gave him command of a body of horse.

This young man was none other than Haider Ali, who, later, was destined to play so important a part in the wars with the English.

Haider increased his force and enriched himself by a system of wholesale plunder, most of which he expended on the payment of his men. When the country was once more threatened by the Mahrattas, he was sent in command of the army to drive them out. He returned victorious, and was received by the Hindu Rajah and his minister with great honour. It took but a short time for Haider to show himself in his true colours. Gradually he assumed the government of the state and obliged the minister to retire. His ambition had no limit; he extended his conquests until he came in touch with the English whom he believed he could drive back into the sea.

From that period, 1760, to the beginning of the nineteenth century Haider, and his son Tippu

A MAHRATTA BRAHMAN GIRL, PROBABLY FROM TANJORE

Her sari is of rich soft silk. She has in her hand a wreath of marigolds made by stringing the heads of the flowers close together.

after him, were in constant collision with the English. There is no doubt that Haider was a genius. He stands out as a soldier autocrat, a leader of men, paying his troops and carrying them on from victory to victory until his name became a terror throughout the peninsula. Tanjore, Trichinopoly, Madura, even Madras itself trembled at the thought of the Mysorean Horse, fierce unscrupulous mounted men, who appeared without warning, looted towns and villages, and then rode off as suddenly as they came, leaving desolation and death behind them.

It was during these troublous times that the villagers surrounded their villages with the thorn hedges mentioned by historians. The hedges were 30 feet wide, planted thickly with the Mysore thorn, bamboo, and cactus. Here the wretched cultivators found shelter while their fields were wantonly destroyed and their cattle driven off. They lived a precarious life, not daring to go far afield, and ploughing with the weapons of defence close at hand. The harassed people were praying for a deliverer when the English determined that in the interests of trade and agriculture the power of the Mysore usurper must be broken. It was a hard nut to crack, for Haider was no mean foe, and reverses were in store for the attacking power before the end was accomplished.

Haider Ali died in 1782. He was succeeded by his son Tippu Sultan, a man of strange character, who inherited some of his father's qualities, with an admixture of a Nero-like brutality on one hand and a love of art and letters on the other. The brutality took the form of pleasure in the sight of bloodshed and suffering, pain and death. Men armed with lancet weapons fastened on their hands were pitted against each other, and made to continue the fight long after one of them had been vanquished. Elephants, tigers, buffaloes, and rams were goaded on to struggle with each other till death put an end to the contest. The most terrible of all the shows this monster delighted in was the crushing of human beings under the feet of elephants. In the old palace in the fort at Bangalore the dais is still shown where Tippu sat to see this horrible sight. It is in the form of a gigantic bracket, and access to it was by way of the verandah of the harem; for he stood in constant fear of the assassin's knife. The elephants were trained to pursue and crush with their feet.

Old natives living in Trichinopoly, Bangalore, and Madras in 1880 could remember the tales they had heard as children from the lips of their grandparents of the terrible deeds of Tippu, the Tiger of Mysore as they called him, and of the sights that the old people themselves had witnessed in their youth.

His ill fame and the report of his cruelty to the English prisoners who fell into his hands spread throughout the whole of British India; and when he was finally besieged and brought to bay at Seringapatam the issue was watched in Bombay and Calcutta as well as Madras with the utmost anxiety. General Harris, the Commander-in-Chief of the Madras Army, afterwards Lord Harris, was in command of the expedition.

Before attacking the fort General Harris gave Tippu the opportunity of capitulating. A man of that kind, who had shown no mercy, was not likely to look for mercy at the hands of an enemy with whom he had dealt treacherously. When the hours passed in silence and no reply was received it was understood that he refused.

On the 4th May 1799, a date against which Tippu had been warned by the astrologers and seers, the assault was made, the fort was taken, and the tyrant and usurper of the Mysore throne was killed as he was attempting to escape to the town. When the storming of the fort began he was at dinner. He immediately got up and armed himself with "sword and fusils." He went to the north rampart and fired several times upon the attacking party. Noticing that his own troops had retired, he asked for his horse and rode towards the sally-port or water-gate. It was crowded, and as he was making his way with difficulty he was wounded by a musket ball. Half-way through the gate he was wounded a second time and the horse also. He dismounted with the help of his servant, and was placed upon his palankeen under the archway. Some European soldiers entered the gateway, and one of them seized his sword-belt to strip it of its buckle, not recognising that it was the sultan himself. Tippu made a cut at him with his sword, but was himself killed by a bullet fired at close quarters which went through his head.

J. J. Cotton, of the Madras Civil Service, in his book on the monuments of the Presidency, attaches a note on the tomb of Mrs. Christenau at St. Mary's, Fort St. George, to the effect that Christenau was said to be the name of the soldier who finally killed Tippu ; he was a man belonging to the Swiss Regiment de Meuron.

Lord Valentia, who visited Colonel de Meuron,

the commandant of the regiment, in 1804 at Seringapatam, wrote: "It is still unknown who gave the fatal wound to the sultaun. The invaluable string of pearls he wore round his neck was the prize of the soldier; but it has never been produced and traced. He (Tippu) had been many years collecting this, always taking off an inferior pearl when he could purchase one of more value."

The Christenau family never showed any sign of possessing great and unusual wealth. They settled in South India and remained in a position suitable to a pensioner in the Company's service.

Tippu was accompanied by a trusted servant named Rajah Khan, who was wounded and fell with his master, but was not killed. It is possible that he may have taken the pearls and any other jewels Tippu might have been wearing to give them to his sons the young princes. As more than a century has elapsed since the loss it is unlikely that the mystery of their disappearance will ever be solved.

It was necessary for political reasons that Tippu's body should be found and identified. He was discovered under a heap of dead in the gateway where he fell. His turban was missing, and the only ornament he wore was an amulet fastened upon his arm. It contained a brittle metallic substance and a charm written in Arabic and Persian.

Thus the Tiger of Mysore died in the very place where he, and his father before him, had confined and brutally ill-treated so many English prisoners of war.

The mention of these unfortunates and all that they suffered still stirs the indignation of those who read the records. They were fettered, half-starved, subjected to all manner of indignities, and only the hardiest survived. Many were compelled to drink poison; others died lingering deaths by starvation or disease. Comparatively few lived to have their fetters struck off. Freedom came, however, to the miserable remnant before the death of the tyrant. Their release was one of the conditions of the peace concluded in 1784. Their feelings when release came can be best described in the actual words written by one of them: "While we were in this gloomy state of mind, and ready to sink under the pressure of melancholy and black despair, behold! a Bramin was sent from Tippu Sultaun with a formal intimation of the conclusion of peace!—and that our irons were to be knocked off next day. The emotions that sprang up in our breasts on receiving this intelligence were so strong and lively, and raised to such a point of elevation and excess as almost bordered on pain! The whole prison resounded with the frantic voice of sudden as well as excessive joy and exultation."

The prisoners consulted together how they could best celebrate the event. There was no longer any need to economise the dole allowed them by Tippu. It was a mean pittance, barely sufficient to provide them with enough food to keep them alive. Millet and coarse rice was all they could afford. Such luxuries as coffee and fruit were beyond their means, and the consoling pipe impossible.

They decided to pool their cash and spend it all on bananas and sherbet and make a feast. They were as merry over it as though it were a rich banquet; and they toasted the friends they hoped to see again before long in sherbet. They had little or no sleep that night, and daylight was awaited with the utmost impatience.

Their fetters, heavy iron manacles, were riveted upon their limbs. The help of skilled workmen was required to remove them. From dawn their ears were alert for sounds of their coming, and the hours dragged wearily. At seven a single armourer appeared. He was instantly besieged by the impatient prisoners, and it was difficult for him to know where to begin. It was not until three o'clock in the afternoon that his work was done and the last man set free.

Now came an unexpected difficulty. They had been so long accustomed to dragging a heavy weight as they walked, they found it impossible to move with any freedom; and it was some time before they could throw off the impression that their ankles were chained.

They were conducted under an escort to the killedar to receive their permits to depart. As they crossed the parade-ground a number of European boys in Muhammadan dress came to them and implored them to use their influence to obtain a release.

It is to be feared that the English boys were forgotten. They were taken in a sea-fight by the French Admiral Suffrein and were handed over by him to Haider, a piece of superfluous carelessness that will for ever be a stain upon the admiral's name. It is said that there were as many as a hundred of these boys; it is possible that the military authorities and the peace commissioners may not have known of their existence.

Seringapatam is full of historical associations, not only connected with the rise and fall of these Mysore princes, but also with British officers whose names are well known in history. The greatest is that of the Duke of Wellington, then Colonel Arthur Wellesley. He lived in Tippu's favourite palace after the death of the Tiger. It was called the Darya Daulat Bagh. The walls were covered with paintings representing the defeat of the English under the unfortunate Colonel Baillie in 1780 by Haider Ali. Seven hundred Europeans and five thousand sepoys were killed or taken prisoner on that occasion, with guns and ammunition, tents, and stores. It was one of the worst disasters that ever happened to the British arms in India. The cruel sports that found so much favour in the eyes of Tippu used to take place in front of this palace.

Seringapatam was garrisoned by Europeans for a few years subsequent to its fall; but the place proved unhealthy, being frequently visited by cholera. As soon as the country was sufficiently settled under the Hindu ruler set up by British authority, the troops moved to Bangalore, which still remains a large military centre.

As an evidence of what cholera can do, Scott's

bungalow may be regarded as an example. It stands by the side of the river Cauvery on the island of Seringapatam. It was occupied by Lieutenant-Colonel L. G. Scott, Commandant of Seringapatam in 1817. His wife and two daughters were with him. They were suddenly seized with cholera which killed all three in a few hours. Scott was stunned by the blow which had fallen on him. He fled from the place, leaving his house as it stood, fully furnished with all the personal properties lying about just as his dear ones had used them. Time and other destructive influences have wrought havoc on the drapery and more perishable things; but the furniture remains.

The tale has been made the subject of some verses by Aliph Cheem (Captain Yeldham) in the *Lays of Ind.* He chants the history of the catastrophe, and gives a graphic description of the bungalow as he saw it about 1880.

A TANK IN MYSORE WITH THE MAHA-RAJAH'S PALACE IN THE DISTANCE

The donkeys carry loads of soiled linen to be washed. The trees are preserved by masonry embankments because they are sacred to some demon, worshipped once a year or in times of scarcity or sickness by the village people.

CANARESE AND GIPSIES

Take care not to fix your abode in a place where there is no temple, no headman, no school, no river, no astrologer, and no doctor.

Niti Sloka, lix. (Dubois).

CANARESE WOMAN GRINDING MILLET (RAGI)

It is boiled until it thickens, when it is made into unleavened dumplings which are eaten cold or hot with a pepper relish. The woman is showing a dumpling in her hand.

CHAPTER XVII

CANARESE AND GIPSIES

THE language of Mysore is Canarese. Tamil and Telugu may also be heard, and Hindustani is spoken by the Muhammadans. There are many castes, including outcastes among the Canarese; and they have different forms of the Hindu religion. The hill tribes, like those of the Nilgiris, are animists and worship the spirits of the forest, otherwise devils in trees, stones, and streams. Curious customs prevail among certain castes of the Canarese, showing the influence of the Muhammadan rulers, Haider Ali and Tippu Sultan. The Bedars who worship Hindu deities practise circumcision. Haider's army was largely recruited from the tribe, and the Semitic rite may have been forced upon them. In these days they make excellent police constables and revenue peons.

A curious custom, which has been put down by

Government, prevailed among another caste of Canarese. Before betrothing and piercing the ears of the eldest daughter of a family the mother was obliged to submit to the amputation of the third and little fingers of the right hand. The operation was crudely performed by the village blacksmith, who chopped off the fingers with his chisel. There was no object in so barbarous a rite; it was therefore very properly forbidden by the authorities, and is no longer practised.

The Canarese are an industrious people whether employed in the fields or otherwise. They grow ragi and cholum (millets), rice and two kinds of gram that may be respectively likened to peas and beans. Ragi, cholum, and gram are ground into flour that thickens in the cooking like pea flour. Ground or whole, it is boiled until soft, and then it is kneaded into puddings that have no attraction as a rule for the English palate. Sir Mountstuart Grant-Duff, when he was Governor of Madras, had a liking for ragi cakes, made like oatmeal cakes and served hot for breakfast. The boiled ragi is eaten with a highly seasoned relish in the shape of a curry or chutney or a thick kind of peppery gruel called dhall.

The woman who has been grinding the grain

holds in her hand one of these puddings which she has brought with her for the midday meal.

The Canarese do not eat much rice; it is not their staple food. On the other hand the rice-eating natives from the plains cannot assimilate the ragi in any quantity. It was one of the difficulties in feeding the people of South India in the great famine to provide them with the grain to which they were accustomed.

The saris of the women are red or blue, the latter tint prevailing. The deep indigo harmonises with the colour of the landscape, the blue-green of the forest-covered hills and the azure of the distant peaks. Living in a sub-tropical climate on the plateau the Canarese compare favourably in physique with the Tamils of the plains. They are less susceptible to cold and damp, and are capable of greater endurance.

The forest tribes of the Western Ghats have a wonderful power of walking long distances. They travel barefooted, taking a wide stride with a springing action and a bending of the knees. The body swings forward free of jerk, and there is no waste of energy. Seen from a distance the stride appears to result in a slow deliberate pace; but if a European attempts to follow a Canarese or a hillman up the side of a mountain, he soon finds himself out-distanced and winded into the bargain.

The man most noted for his travelling capacity is the Indian Gipsy, the Brinjara or Lambani—or Lumbadi as he is better known in Mysore. He is of a dark complexion, but there is nothing negroid about his features, they are well formed; and the women have long black hair that they wear in ringlets or plaits. Into the plaits they weave shells as ornaments, and the ends are finished off with red cotton tassels. Their dress is picturesque and entirely different from the costumes of the races among whom they live. Ornaments of brass, bone, and shells adorn neck and arms, and over the head is drawn an embroidered mantle such as the woman in the sketch is wearing.

Their past history is not known, and their origin can only be conjectured. They speak a dialect called Kutni, which is composed to a great extent of the Hindi and Mahratta languages.

The Indian Gipsies are great thieves; this woman was under close police surveillance, not for any crime she had committed, but for what she might commit if allowed to wander at large near

A WOMAN OF THE TRIBE OF INDIAN GIPSIES KNOWN AS LUMBADEES

The artist says: "This nomad tribe wanders about Mysore and the Western Ghats. They possess a sturdy race of bullocks which they use for transport. Although they are great thieves they are scrupulously honest over any goods entrusted to their charge for porterage. I found this woman locked up in a railed enclosure near the police station. As far as I could make out she was not there for any crime she had committed. The police had received orders to keep their eye upon her, and this in their opinion was the best method of carrying out their instructions. I had some difficulty in persuading the authorities to allow her to come to my tent to be sketched."

the Governor's camp. To make everything secure, the police had locked her up; and Lady Lawley had great difficulty in persuading them to allow her to come to the camp to be sketched.

The Lumbadis possess large herds of bullocks, which they use for transport purposes. The bullocks are as sturdy and strong as their owners, and prove themselves as nimble as goats on the steep, rough tracks of the mountains.

Although notoriously light-fingered, the Lumbadis keep faith, as a rule, with their patrons, and will deliver intact any goods committed to their charge. They were largely used in the Mysore and Mahratta wars by both sides to convey rice for the armies. Forty thousand bullocks were supplied for transport purposes to the English in the Mysore campaigns and thirty-five thousand to the Duke of Wellington, then General Wellesley, in the Mahratta War.

Captain John Briggs—afterwards General Sir John—in a paper on the "Bunjaras" or Indian Gipsies, published in the *Transactions of the Literary Society*, Bombay, 1819, relates two instances of infidelity in their contracts with the British army. One incident is worthy of mention because of its relation to the Duke of Wellington.

A clan or tanda—as the Lumbadi clans are called—was commissioned to convey grain for the British troops. Some doubt must have existed as to the faith that would be kept, for Dooly Khan, an officer commanding a body of the Nizam's Horse and an ally of the English, caught the Lumbadis in the act of going over to the enemy.

Dooly Khan reported the circumstance to Wellington, who wrote in reply, ordering the grain to be confiscated and the headman or Naick of the tanda to be hung.

The first part of the order was promptly fulfilled; but for some reason, unstated, the punishment of the Gipsy Naick was not carried out, and he escaped.

Five years later this very man had the impudence to approach Lieutenant-Colonel Barclay, who had been Adjutant-General with Colonel Wellesley in the Deccan, with a petition. He complained that Dooly Khan had seized and appropriated a large quantity of grain from him, and that no payment had been made. Colonel Barclay was taken in by the plausibility of the Naick, and espoused his cause. He wrote to a friend at Hyderabad and asked him to use his influence with the Resident, Captain Thomas

A CANARESE WOMAN DRAWING WATER

The circlet on the top of her head is made of dried grass. The pot rests upon it when she carries the water home.

Sydenham. The friend accordingly introduced the Naick and told the tale of his supposed wrongs.

At that time Dooly Khan was living in Hyderabad. Captain Sydenham sent for him with the intention of making him pay the Naick his debt. The officer came, and the Gipsy Naick was called in. Dooly Khan recognised him at once, and, moreover, readily admitted that he had appropriated the grain for the use of his troops.

"I have an order about me to hang that old man," he said.

Thereupon he took off his turban and drew from the folds a number of letters. Among them was General Wellesley's. He handed it to Captain Sydenham, who at once saw the affair in a different light. He pointed out to the Naick that he had had a fortunate escape, and that he would be wise if he said nothing more about his claim, since the death sentence still remained uncancelled by reprieve or pardon. The Naick retired without a word.

Captain Sydenham turned to Dooly Khan and inquired how it was that he carried the letter with him, as he could not have been aware of the object for which he had been summoned to the Residency. Dooly Khan replied:

"You see, sir, in that packet every letter I ever received from General Wellesley. I keep them always close to my person, or on my head, out of respect for the military talents and capacity of a man whose equal I never saw either as a soldier or politician; and while I possess these, I am convinced I shall meet with no harm; they are, in fact, a talisman."

Of late years, with the introduction of railways, the transport trade of the Lumbadis has declined. Some of the clans have settled down, building themselves wicker huts of the gipsy tent description. Some of them have accepted regular work on coffee and tea estates in Coorg and Mysore. Others look to the forest for their livelihood, like the Kurumbas, bringing in firewood and other products for sale in the towns and villages.

For the people living out of reach of road and rail they are as necessary as ever, carrying salt and salt fish from the coast, and taking back whatever the villagers may have to offer. In former days sandalwood was smuggled by aid of the Lumbadis from Mysore to the west coast. For a long time they evaded the police; their knowledge of the hill paths enabled them to pass up and down the mountains without being caught. A well-timed raid made some years ago ended in the seizure of a very large consignment of contraband stuff and the confiscation of a number of bullocks. The traffic was broken, and though it may be carried on in a small way here and there—the Lumbadis are ever ready to lend themselves to irregularities of this kind—the smuggling no longer continues on a large scale.

Like the English Gipsies the Lumbadis have their own dogs, a peculiar breed of long-limbed, powerful animals. They are brown or grey, and are not unlike the Poligar dogs of the plains in the south, except that the latter have less hair. They attach themselves strongly to their masters; but with strangers they are shy and unfriendly, taking after their wolf ancestors. The Indian dog of the plains is said to be descended from the jackal, a less courageous progenitor. The Poligar dog makes a fine hunting dog. Probably the Indian Gipsies find the same good quality in their own animals.

If the Lumbadis have a weakness other than being light-fingered, it is their fondness for strong drink. They celebrate all their festivals by deep potations of a coarse, fiery arrack. As these orgies take place in the depths of the forest, they give offence to no one. The native, whether he belongs to the hills or the plains, is rarely turbulent and vicious in his cups, if he confines himself to arrack. On the other hand, if he indulges in any of the poisonous decoctions of hemp and datura that are brewed, he becomes nothing less than a raving maniac, liable to run amok at any moment.

The visitor to Southern India cannot fail to be struck with the quiet contentment that is to be found among the people. It is not a joyous, conscious contentment, such as might be shown by human beings who had attained the dearest wishes of their hearts. It is rather the placid contentment of a people who have been relieved from a long reign of oppression and suffering—of a peaceful people who have lived for ages in fear of the plundering freebooter, from whom at length they are freed. Under British rule every man may plough his field in peace and carry his goods to market in safety. The people are aware of the boon they enjoy, and they are satisfied and contented.

The yoke is where the gods place it.

In the present day it is so placed in the south that it is not felt.

INDEX

Aaron, 72
Abraham, 71, 72
Acacia melanoxylon, 212
Adam and Eve, 53
Afflatus, the divine, 130, 145
Afghan, 9, 17
Agent creeper, 196
Agni, 220
Ali, Prophet's son-in-law, 60, 62, 63
Aliph Cheem, 240
Allah, names of, 52
All-Father, 129
Almsgiving, 59, 103
Amma, 139
Amulet, 85, 202, 235
Angels, 73, 99, 103
Animist, 10, 129, 137
Antichrist, 97
Arab, 9
Arabian Nights, 207
Arcot, Prince of, 29
Armenian, 9
Arrack, 147
Artisans, 114
Artists, 48
Aryan, 108, 109
Astrologer, 36, 133
Australia, 212
Ayesha, 48

Baillie, Colonel, 239
Bangalore, 232
Banqueting Hall, 17
Banyan tree, 4, 123
Barclay, Lieut.-Colonel, 248
Bedar, 243
Bell, Dr., 125
Bhagavad-Gita, 122
Bodyguard, 6
Books of the East, 121
Books, palm-leaf, 124
Bowani River, 192
Boys, English, at devil-dance, 143
Brahma, 96, 137
Brahman, 3, 4, 9, 108, 111, 112, 130, 132, 153, 158
Bride, Muhammadan, 37, 44
Bridge to Heaven, 103
Briggs, Sir J., 247
Brinjara, 246 (*see* Lumbadi)
Buchanan, Dr. F., 192
Budaga, 205, 206
Buddhist, 10
Buqr'Id feast, 71
Burial-ground, 149
Burmese, 9
Butler at Government House, 6

Caldwell, Bishop, 186
Canarese, 199, 211, 226, 240, 245
Cape, the, 193
Caste, 7, 8, 107, 153, 159
Cauvery River, 141, 240
Cemeteries, 98, 101
Ceylon, 134, 149
Chandra Mahdi, 177
Charm, 76 (*see* Amulet)

Chepauk, 29
Child, Muhammadan, 31
Cholera, 239
Christenau, 234
Christian, 54
Christianity, 137
Chuhra, 158
Chuttrum, 124
Circumcision, 243
Coimbatore, 193
Contentment of people, 252
Cooking, 166
Coonoor, 194, 204
Coorg, 250
Cooum River, 5, 15
Cotton, Mr. J. J., 234
Creepers, 196
Curry, making, 166

Dances, devil. *See* Devil-dancer
Dances, village, 181
Dancing girl, 131
Darnell, Ralph, 218
Darya Doulat Bagh, 239
David, 83
Day, Last, 97
Days, unlucky, 77
Deccan, 88
Delhi, 228
De Meuron, Colonel, 234
Demon, 83, 138, 140, 145, 146, 148
Derwish, 89, 90
Deva dasi, 131
Devil, cast out, 84
Devil-chariots, 143
Devil-dancer, 137, 144, 147
Devil-mask, 149
Devil-stone, 126, 127
Devils, 129, 138, 140
Disease, 83, 85, 86
Doctor, native, 83
Dodabetta, 207, 218
Dooly Khan, 248
Dravidian, 76, 109
Durga pujah, 66
Dussera, 66

East India Company, 15, 191, 192
Ebony of the ancients, 195
Education, 126
Elementals, 139
Elias, 72
English, 25, 187
Enoch, 74
Eucalyptus, 211
Eugenics, 54
European, 191
Evil eye, 86, 165
Excellency, His, 7
Exorcism, 84, 140

Fable on luck, 87
Fakir, 22, 88, 89, 91
Fakir's tomb, 92
Feudal system, 113
Fights, animal, 179, 180
Figures, magic, 138
Fingers, amputation of, 244
Forest, 194, 196, 197, 203
Forest fire, 219
Fort St. George, 15, 115, 234
French, the, 16, 29
Furniture, Hindu, 163
Futhoomu, 83
Future state, 104

Gabriel, the angel, 54, 72, 74
Games, village, 180, 181, 182
Ganesa, 129
Ganges, 66
Garden, 15, 161
Garden House, 16, 17
Georgetown, 115
Ghats, Western, 191, 195, 205, 245
Ghosts, 99
Giants, white, 207
Gipsy, 246 (*see* Lumbadi)
Gneiss, 226
Gosha, 32
Government House, 4, 6, 15
Governor, the, 6, 7, 8
Grain, 244
Grant-Duff, Sir M., 244
Grass-cutter, 213
Gum tree, 211
Guru, 111

Hagar, 71
Haider Ali, 217, 230, 232, 243
Hakim, 85
Hanuman, 129
Hardwar, 22
Harris, Lord, 233
Harut, 74
Hawkers, 5
Heaven, 103
Hell, 97, 100, 104
Hemp, 91
Herklots, Dr., 77
Heyne, Dr., 114
Hindu, 9, 10, 65, 96, 110, 111, 123, 124, 161, 163, 165, 246
Hoolicul Droog, 217, 225
Horoscope, 36
House, Hindu, 161, 163, 165
House, Muhammadan, 29
Husain and Hasan, 60, 61, 62
Hyderabad, 88, 248
Hypnotism, 20, 140

Imam, 99
Incantation, 140
Innovation forbidden, 49
Ishmael, 71
Israel, 74
Israfel, 74, 97

Jesus Christ, 97, 100, 138
Jew, 53
Jinn, 73, 83, 99

Kali, 130
Kindersley, 192, 194
King-Emperor, 11
Kismet, 86
Kitchen, 161, 162
Kota, 205
Krishna, 130, 139
Kshattriya, 108, 112
Kufa, 61
Kundah Hills, 216
Kurumba, 199, 203, 206, 250
Kutni, 246

Lally, 16
Lamp, lighting of, 165
Lawley, Sir A., and Lady, 6, 24, 62, 148, 202, 247
Lays of Ind, 240
Legion, 138
Lumbadi or Lumbani, 194, 246, 248, 251
Lushington, Stephen, 194

Madras, 115, 231
Madura, 115, 231
Magic, 77, 85
Magician, 77, 115, 127, 140
Mahabharata, 122
Mahratta, 9, 228, 246
Manu, 107, 109, 112
Markanda, 178
Market, 182, 183
Marriage, 34, 41, 43
Marut, 74
Maternity, 166
Michael, 74
Mimosa, 212
Mirage, 142
Moghul, 228, 229
Moses, 53, 72
Mosque, 57, 65
Mount road, 6, 17, 29, 92
Muavia, 60
Muckwa, 9
Muezzin, 56, 57
Muhammad, 48, 54, 55
Muhammadan, 4, 10, 59, 70, 107, 131
Muhammadan children, 45, 46
Muhammadan faith, 53, 58, 99
Muhammadan festivals, 66, 71
Muhammadan funeral, 99, 101
Muhammadan superstitions, 76
Muhammadan wives, 43
Muharram, 60
Mullah, 36, 41, 72
Munkir, 98, 102, 103
Musician, 144, 176
Myliapur, 18
Mysore, 191, 199, 211, 225, 226, 231, 243
Mystics, 89

Nakir, 98, 102, 103
Nawab of Carnatic, 17
Nilgiri Hills, 191, 194, 199, 206
Noah, 72

Occupation, Hindu, 166
Occupation, Muhammadan, 31
Odd numbers, 56
Oil mill and cart, 227
Omar Khayyam, 91
Ootacamund, 193, 194, 211, 215, 216
Outcastes, 113, 116, 159

Palmyra tree, 142
Panch, 157
Panchalar, 153
Pandian kings, 186
Pandian, T. B., 115
Paradise, 97, 113
Pariah, 113, 158
Patriarchs, 53
Patterns on doorsteps, 164
Pennell, Dr., 22
Peon, 148
Pial school, 123
Pillars of Islam, 55
Pitt, 16
Poet, 121, 123, 174
Poligar dogs, 251
Polyandry, 203
Poor, the, 60
Portia tree, 4
Possession, 140, 141
Prayer, 55-58, 100, 101
Priest, 111
Prisoners, English, 233, 236
Professions, Hindu, 114
Pujah, 127
Pujari, 127, 132, 141, 160
Punchama, 3
Punchayet, 167
Pupil teachers, 125
Purohit, 111
Purushu, 107, 109

Qanun-i-Islam, 76
Qazi, 41, 42, 43
Quarrels, religious, 65
Quran, 22, 43, 53, 56, 97

Rajah Hari Chandra, 177
Rajah Khan, 235
Rajanya, 112
Ramaswami Raju, 87
Ramayana, 122
Ramazan, 55, 59, 71
Religion, respect for, 11, 23
Religious rites, 159
Resurrection, the, 97
Rijal ul Gyb, 79
Rishika, 22
Royapettah, 35
Rupee, 49

Sacrifice, blood, 141, 148, 202, 205
Sacrifice, human, 202
Sadhu, 18, 19, 22, 23, 24, 25, 89
St. Thome, 17
Salaam, the, 102
Salaams, feast of, 72
Sanyasi, 21, 22, 25, 91
Schoolmaster, 123, 125
Schools, Civil and Military, 125
Scott, Colonel L. G., 240
Seer, 160
Sell, Canon, 59, 66, 90
Seringapatam, 233, 239
Sewing machine, 185
Shahdi marriage, 43
Shahji, 228
Shanar caste, 143
Shandy, 182
Sharrock, Rev. J. A., 110
Shiahs, 62, 66
Shopkeeper, 184
Shraddah ceremonies, 160
Shytan, 73, 76
Sicily, 191
Sikhs, 11, 158
Singhalese, 9
Siva, 11, 66, 130, 139, 178, 179
Sivaji, 228
Smuggling by Lumbadis, 250
Solomon, 83

Spirits, 137, 139, 146
Srirungam, 128, 132
Standards, Muhammadan, 63
Street characters, 8, 9, 10
Strolling players, 174
Stylus, 124
Subramanian, 132
Sudra, 108, 113, 141
Suffrein, Admiral, 238
Sufi, 90, 91, 96
Sullivan, Mr. John, 193
Sunnis, 62, 66
Sweeper, 158
Syce, 213
Sydenham, Captain, 249

Tabut procession, 62, 63
Taj Mahal, 49
Tamarind, 4, 123
Tanjore, 115, 229, 231
Tantras, 122
Taylor, Meadows, 218
Taziah, 63
Temple, Hindu, 126, 148
Temple-building, 128
Testament, Old, 54
Theatre, village, 175
Thomas, Mr., I.C.S., 212
Tinnevelly, 143
Tippu Sultan, 217, 232, 234, 235, 243
Toda, 203-6
Toddy-drawer, 143
Tomtoms, 145
Trades, 113, 114
Traditions, the, 56
Transmigration, 95
Trichinopoly, 115, 128, 132, 140, 231
Triplicane, 17, 25, 29, 59, 62, 76, 92
Tuticorin, 17

Upanishad, 122

Vaisya, 108, 112
Valentia, Lord, 234
Valluvan, 5, 21, 22, 136
Vedas, 107, 112
Vellala caste, 141
Vellore temple, 65
Venus, 75
Vijayanagar, 228
Village amusements, 173, 179
Village council, 167
Village Court, 167
Village independence, 169
Village system, 113, 169, 184, 185
Vishnu, 10, 130, 139

Wallajah road, 18
Wattle, 212
Wellesley, Sir A., 239, 247
Wellington, Duke of, 239
Wellington, military depôt, 204
Were-tiger and leopard, 200
Whish, Mr., 192, 194
Widow, Hindu, 35
Wodiga, 10
Women's seclusion, 30, 31

Xavier, 10

Yale, 16
Yeldham, Captain, 240
Yezid, 61
Yoga, 20, 22, 90

Zuhra, 75

THE END

SKETCH MAP OF SOUTHERN INDIA

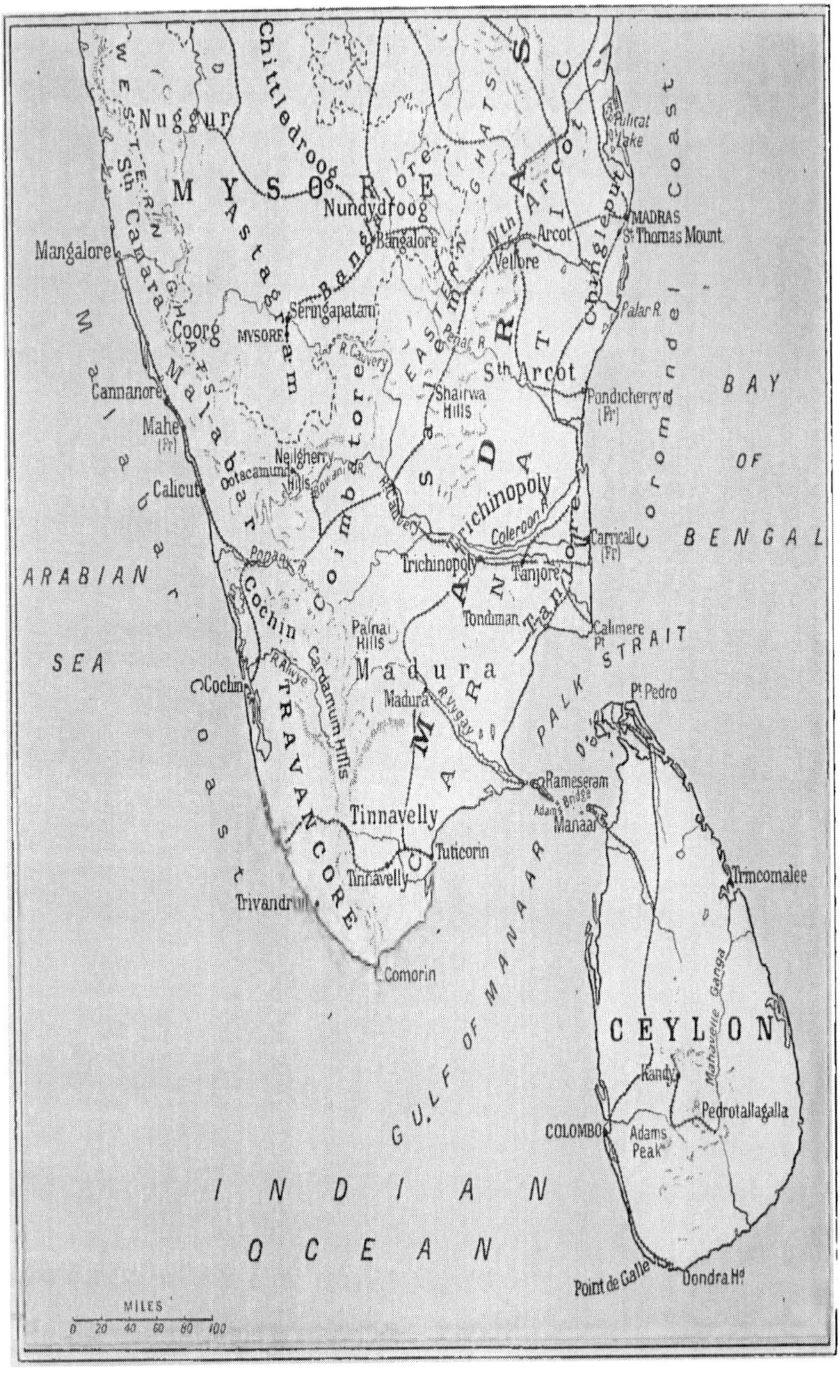

ACCOMPANYING "SOUTHERN INDIA" BY LADY LAWLEY AND MRS. F. E. PENNY. PUBLISHED BY A. & C. BLACK, LONDON.